On the day when he was to paint he would seat himself by a bright window, put his desk in order, burn incense to his right and left, and place good brushes and excellent ink beside him; then he would wash his hands and rinse his ink-well, as if to receive an important guest, thereby calming his spirit and composing his thoughts. Not until then did he begin to paint.

SSU, a Sung painter, speaking of his father. (From *An Essay on Landscape Painting*, by Kuo Hsi, translated by Shio Sakanishi. Published by John Murray).

But all these reasons are only excuses, and paint ideas are significant only if they are the outcome of painting, coming at the end and not at the beginning. The preliminary idea, no matter how insistent, must be broken down, superseded. So then I put on my painting boots. For you see, painting is something—rather distasteful, like cleaning out the drains; and sitting in the paint (which one must do) and standing in the picture (which one must do) . . . a messy business.

ALAN DAVIE *Towards a New Definition of Art* (By kind permission of 'New Departures').

You are an artist
A practical approach to art
by Fred Gettings
Paul Hamlyn

I dedicate this book to the twenty-odd children who, anxious to learn about art, used to wreck my studio once a week. And to Sheila, who used to put up with it.

First published 1965
2nd impression 1967
3nd impression 1968

Published by
The Hamlyn Publishing Group Limited
Hamlyn House · The Centre · Feltham · Middlesex
© Paul Hamlyn 1965
Printed in Czechoslovakia

Contents

Preface

The aim of this book is to show that you *are* an artist.
Art is not concerned merely with great artists, with genius
or with prodigious skills. It is, fundamentally, the outward
form of an inward search. To participate in this search, on
whatever level and with whatever ability, is to be an artist.
The equipment of the artist is not found in art shops only,
but in his attitude of mind, in his vision and in his emotions.
It is of supreme unimportance whether the artist is
possessed of some dazzling vision, like Samuel Palmer in the
valley of Shoreham, or whether he paints almost as a matter
of amusement with whatever materials that happen to be at
hand, like old Alfred Wallis of St Ives – the important thing,
the thing which links all artists together, is the search.

Works of art, sometimes good and sometimes bad, are the
outward evidence of this search. But the work of art is really
of secondary importance – it is merely the crystallisation
of an idea or emotion, and a correct understanding of
art must take this fact into account. The true importance of
art lies in its alchemical nature, in its strange power to
refine the sensibilities, to heighten visual awareness. This
evolution of the spirit is the true aim of art, and anyone who
embarks on this spiritual odyssey bears the name of artist.
The practice of art is not directed towards producing artists
who can paint or sculpt with real ability, nor towards
producing more works to fill our homes and galleries: it is
directed towards producing human beings with a sense of
wonder at life and that precious ability to enquire into its
outward manifestations.

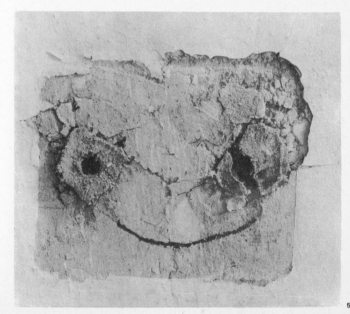

Introduction

6

In childhood there is little thought of the impermanence of things. As a child one can scribble in coloured chalks on pavements and watch one's pictures being washed away in the rain, or one can make models out of plasticine or snow and then reshape the creations on the following day. With adults this attitude towards art is more rare. Michelangelo is supposed to have sculpted in snow, and Cézanne would often throw away his pictures when they were finished, whilst at least one modern artist burns her constructions as part of the 'creative act'; but these are exceptional cases in the history of art. Behind the activity of almost every artist there lies a need to create something lasting, a wish to give emotions or ideas a permanent form.

As soon as a child wants to keep his paintings 'to show to Mummy', his days of childhood art are over: he loses interest in the act of creation and finds a new and perhaps pernicious interest in the end product. Perhaps it is this change from childhood to adulthood that artists such as Klee and Miro have in mind when they urge us to paint like little children. Perhaps they mean we should try to develop or rediscover that lost attitude to art in which the actual creative act, the experiment, the solving of problems, are more important than the result or the solution.

Freud said that every one of us is an artist in our dreams. We are all of us artists in our imagination, for it is imagination coloured by knowledge which produces a work of art. The actual making of a picture – the business of arranging paint on a surface of canvas – is not as important as the act of imagination which gave rise to the picture in the first place. The creative act lies in the visualisation of the finished thing. The picture may be conceived in a flash of imagination and then executed, or it may develop through a series of successive acts of imagination at different stages of the painting, but always it is the power of imagination which is the controlling element. The wall texture in plate 4 is purely accidental, but it requires only one single line (plate 15) to transform it into a very expressive face. Quite obviously it was not the act of drawing the line which turned the texture into a work of art: it was that power of imagination which saw in the texture its visual possibilities.

Art for Art's sake is a very good principle, if, as Chesterton

puts it, 'it means that there is a vital distinction between the earth and the tree that has its roots in the earth; but it is a very bad principle if it means that the tree could grow just as well with its roots in the air.' Art is of more value for the way it improves the mind and sensibilities than for its end products.

There is a story of a Chinese artist who painted his pig asleep in its sty and then proudly showed the picture to a friend. 'What is it?' the painter asked. 'A dead pig, of course,' came the reply. The artist returned home a trifle disappointed and tried again to paint his sleeping pig, but once more his friend thought it was a picture of a dead pig. After several attempts all with the same comment from his friend the painter devoted all his spare time to studying the pig. He examined it from every angle and under every condition, filling many sketchbooks with drawings of it, gradually spending less and less time actually painting and more time observing it. Eventually he gave up painting altogether and devoted all his spare time to watching the pig. At last he sat down and without so much as another glance at his pig he painted a picture of it asleep. Once more he showed the picture to his friend and asked 'What is it?' 'Why!' said the friend in astonishment, 'it's your pig asleep in his sty!'

The story holds the key to the meaning of art and art history. A work of art is a record of understanding, and the history of art is the history of how man's visual awareness of the world has changed through the ages. Each work of art is the outward form of the artist's personal understanding of the world, and the greatest works of art are the manifestation of men's understanding at its highest level. But art is not the prerogative of great artists: it is an activity in which we may all participate at our different levels, each of us bringing to art what we have – our technical ability and our imagination – and taking from art what we learn.

There are no laws governing art. The creative act is a many-sided, indefinable thing which may appear as an expected grace through contemplation, or tear savagely down like a scream in the night. Creation may be born of an intolerable tension pent up in the mind and soul of a genius racked with pain on a scaffold in the Sistine Chapel, or it

may trickle through the fingers of a rug maker in some remote village. The artist is a delicate instrument manipulated by some immense spirit, and how he manifests his inspiration cannot be subjected to rules.

In early times, it was held that inspiration in all its forms was sacred. The violent jibberish of the lunatic and the inspiration of the genius were recognised as springing from a common womb. Today this common origin is still recognised, but its name has been changed: what was once regarded as a gift of the gods is now ascribed to 'subconscious workings', but still the mysterious act of creation is not understood. In essence art is still the semi-divine, semi-barbarous participation in a natural rhythm that it was twenty thousand years ago in the caves of Lascaux.

There are three stages of artistic development. The first stage is marked by the struggle to acquire technique and an independent attitude towards art. The second stage is one of experiment, in which the artist seeks to find what he must express, endeavouring to refine and intensify his vision of the world in order to improve his art. The third stage demands rare qualities, and it is a stage seldom reached by any but the most gifted. It begins at the point where technical proficiency has been acquired, and the artist knows what he wants to say, seeking only the power to communicate directly what he knows. Few men can honestly say, as Picasso has said, 'I do not seek, I find!'

Of these three stages only the first can actually be taught. The student can learn about technique and how to modify some of his attitudes to art, but after this he is completely alone, with only the art of the past and his own sensibility as a guide. At this point he can either move on to the second stage of development and start the search for expression in which every new attempt to produce a work of art is a plunge into the dark, or he can settle down comfortably to turning out pictures.

In the business of learning about art there are many stumbling blocks and many difficulties, but perhaps the most insidious is one that is common to great artists and beginners alike. It is the tendency to paint or sculpt in order to produce a work of art rather than to learn from the actual attempt to create. Too often one sees an artist, who, after a sincere struggle, finally gains recognition

suddenly coming to a standstill in his development. His work, which was formerly the culmination of a struggle, degenerates into a series of clichés, losing its vitality and becoming fit for nothing but buying and selling. If one has no inclination to learn about art there is little point in painting or sculpting. If, however, one wishes to paint or sculpt one must first of all learn how: one is, therefore, a perpetual student, every attempt to produce a work of art being an attempt to learn something new, and not merely to have something to show.

Contrary to general opinion, an art school is not necessarily a good place to learn about art. Examination requirements and the 'audience' of fellow students often lead to a student who paints for results rather than for what he can learn. The chief advantage of an art school is that it provides space, opportunity and, with a good teaching staff, enthusiasm for art. All of these advantages are within reach of a keen student of art in his own home, and it is of considerable comfort to those for whom an art school training is not possible, to learn that many of the finest painters of today are entirely self-taught.

Of course, a good teacher is valuable – but it must be remembered that once he has taught the basic techniques, all that he can do is offer encouragement by way of praise or criticism. The only essential teacher is the past: there is no artistic problem which has not already been solved by a master, and if one can adopt the attitude to the art of the past which regards each picture as the solution to a problem then one has no need for a teacher.

Any approach to art must be prefaced by an analysis of one's own attitude to art. We must drag aside the blanket of prejudice and half-formed concepts about what art should be in order to see art as it is, and this is best done by attempting to formulate what we think about art in clear and simple terms.

A fairly common belief is that art is concerned with beauty. I once showed a young girl of eight the *Crying Child* by Philip Woolard (plate 9) and asked her if she liked it. The girl said 'No!' and when I asked her why, she replied 'Because it isn't beautiful!' Clearly she did not dwell on the question of what beauty is, but already formed in her mind was the idea of beauty as a criterion. She did not

8 Aboriginal bark painters at work. Australian News and Information Bureau

9 Philip Woolard, 'Crying Child.' Author's collection

10 Wooden figure from the Cook Islands. Museum of Ethnology, Munich

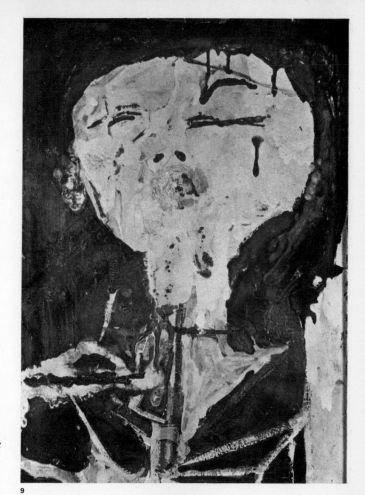

9

consider it possible to like a picture because it is ugly. I spent several minutes talking to her and explaining that the artist had wanted to express the feeling of ugliness and pain of someone crying, and of course the child was quick to appreciate what I said. When I asked her once again if she liked it she said 'Yes, because it's so real!'

The child's first prejudice is very common – many people associate art with beauty without bothering to question the validity of this association. To limit the field of art by referring to the artificial canon of beauty is to reject a whole world of visual experience. Primitive art, for example, can only be understood if we rid ourselves of the idea that it is produced for aesthetic reasons (plate 10).

Another factor which instinctively colours our interpretation when we face a work of art is a belief that every work of art should have a meaning. This is not always so. As we shall see later on, some artists have made excellent works of art by intentionally avoiding any conscious meaning. Oppenheim even lined a teacup with fur and exhibited it as a work of art – without meaning, without function and almost, incidentally, without beauty. Meaning is something which we ourselves attach to an object – it does not exist in the object itself.

Another attitude which often limits the understanding is is the notion that the artist has some secret knowledge. This belief is usually associated with the idea of the artist as a superior being, and it springs from a mistaken sense of the artist's true worth. The artist may know something about the technical side of his work, just as any worker knows something about the technical side of his job, but there is no great mystery to unveil. There are no 'rules' for making works of art, and there are no 'rules' for judging them. The only criteria we have, for creating and for appreciating, exist in our own unique sensibility.

In his excellent book on child art *Scribbling, Drawing and Painting*, Grozinger suggests the harm unwittingly done by parents who continually ask their children what their scribbles are 'about'. That a painting should be 'about something' is a less common sentiment than it used to be, but the old prejudice still persists, and we look for a reference to our familiar world of experience in every work of art, as if this were a suitable yardstick for measuring

10

11

something infinitely greater than ourselves. We must be
wary of this prejudice as much as any other, and seek to
approach art with 'a willing suspension of disbelief' so
that we may be receptive to what it has to teach.

Our aim in learning about art cannot be merely 'to
learn about art'. In an age which takes art – both good and
bad – so ridiculously seriously, it is almost heretical to
suggest that the chief aim of art should be enjoyment.
Enthusiasm and joy can shine through even a bad painting –
whatever the merits or demerits of *Homage to a Clown* at plate
11, it is at least full of joy. A spontaneous joy illuminates
every child's painting or drawing, and is rooted in every
work of genius. The strange drunken epic figure in plate 13
is a work of art only because of the joy it manifests. It
mattered little to the person who created it whether it
turned out to look good or bad: the important thing to him
was the pleasure derived from actually painting the thing.
So many pictures by established painters which are
exhibited nowadays are lacking in the spirit of joy because
they have been painted for an audience with one eye on the
art dealer and the other on accepted canons of taste. The

actual fact of painting, the mystery of participating in an
age-old activity, is too often submerged beneath irrelevant
considerations.

The question of the function of art has never been
satisfactorily answered. Whilst some people suggest that
the creation of a work of art is cathartic, others claim that
it is solely connected with the pleasure impulse in man,
and others see no difference between the two points of view.
The answer to the question surely must lie outside the
relationship of the artist with the created thing, and must
be connected rather with the relationship between the artist
and his audience. The function of art is regeneration of
perception. The artist goes around pointing out new visual
experiences to take the place of the dying ones. The artist
discovers something new in the universe – some new
relationship, some new idea or new fragment or truth – and
he does his best to express his own shock or surprise at this
discovery and to communicate this new perception to an
audience. In this way, what an artist sees is brought into
the common experience of mankind.

The really great artist is a kind of prophet revealing

11 Fred Gettings, 'Homage to a Clown'. Private collection

12 Finger Print, 'Clown' by seven-year-old pupil of Kirtlington Junior School, Oxford. Author's collection

13 'Epic Figure'. Author's studio

hidden truths. He may be described as having 'antennae' which are attuned to sounds beyond the hearing of ordinary men, with a task to represent these hidden things in such a way that ordinary people, those without special antennae, may perceive and understand them.

Of course, there are no such things as 'ordinary people'. Some have long antennae, others short ones, and this, artistically speaking, is the only difference. We are all artists. We may all participate in the search for expression which is such a need in our lives. Art is in the fabric of our very being: it is as natural a process of the spirit as breathing is to the body. No one can be taught to create a work of art for the simple reason that everyone has this ability already. By virtue of being human we are all artists.

Equipment and Materials

14

The traditional image of the artist living in a garret is very much a thing of the past – not merely because even garrets are expensive nowadays, but because the type of bohemianism which is connected with garrets and kippers is no longer in fashion. One is more likely to meet an artist working in an iron foundry with welding equipment or in a basement flat in Soho than in a garret, because a true artist knows that a studio is simply a place to work. A studio may be a corner of one's own living-room or it may be a large barn; it may even be a garret, but provided one has adequate table space, reasonable light and the modicum of materials, other considerations should be of secondary importance.

Obviously the type of work with which you will occupy yourself will be determined by the space and materials you have available. I use one kind of studio (plate 15) for rough work such as casting and for large paintings, and quite a different room (plate 16) for drawing, small watercolour work and delicate modelling. Drawing and painting is difficult enough without complicating matters by having inadequate space and bad light, so one should restrict one's type of work to the facilities available. One constantly meets 'artists' who talk about the wonderful large canvases they would cover if they had the right sort of studio, painfully unaware of their own self-deception. It might be enjoyable to paint 'large' and to have lots of space to make a mess in, but it is simply dishonest to pretend to be an artist and yet not paint because external conditions are not right. How much poorer the world's art would have been if Van Gogh and Gauguin had spent as much time grumbling about the incredible conditions under which they worked instead of getting down to the business of painting pictures.

One could spend a small fortune on the materials and equipment offered in art shops and 'Artist's Materials' catalogues. Here again, unless one can actually afford such luxuries, one may exercise a little self-deception, for one can spend much time and effort in keeping a studio stocked with the most up-to-date furniture and equipment, in keeping all the materials clean and the studio in good order, without actually settling down to paint. It is much more economical, possibly a little more honest, and certainly more enjoyable, to make one's own studio furniture, and utilise all the different materials one can scrounge than to spend an

afternoon in an art shop.

For ordinary work in water colour, gouache and pencil, a table is by far the best easel. It is possible to make or buy a drawing board with adjustable legs which may be placed on a table top and give a firm slope for easy working, but this is not essential. If you do use a drawing board, and you wish to secure your paper, do so with a strip of sticky paper or cellophane, as drawing pins quickly ruin the working surface of your board. If you work directly on to the table top make sure that you cover it completely with newspaper or cheap backing paper in preparation for the inevitable spilled ink.

Work with canvases or canvas boards of any considerable size demands some sort of easel. Oddly enough most of the cheap easels on the market are of little use, for they are not sufficiently firm to hold even a medium sized canvas, and they are not really necessary for small canvases. By far the best easel is the *radial* (plate 17) which has three short legs supporting an upright column which will tilt backwards and forwards as required and which is held in position by a large screw. Along this column two wooden grippers are fixed which may be adjusted to take between them any height of canvas up to eight or nine feet. Two *radial* easels may be used for long canvases, one at either end. This easel is found in most schools, and is a worthwhile investment.

Hardly any easels manufactured especially for out-door use are to be recommended. They are easily blown over, and in spite of their adjustable legs are never very firm. I used one for several years but was eventually reduced to balancing the canvas on my knees.

There is a combined seat-cum-drawing-board-rest on the market which is quite useful, though difficult to store. It is called a 'donkey', and consists of a wooden seat with a wooden beam which projects forward between the legs and supports a vertical T shape in front of the artist upon which a drawing board or canvas may be rested. Many artists use this type of easel with good results, but I find it uncomfortable.

I do not use any kind of commercial easel any more. I have built two very simple easels out of a few pieces of timber and these fulfil my every need. The first is little more than an H shape with a long piece of wood fixed behind the horizontal bar and running parallel to the sides of the H.

5

It is supported by another horizontal bar near the bottom of the H, and along the sides of the H shape I have bored several holes at three-inch intervals into which pegs may be inserted to hold the canvas. The whole apparatus is propped against one of the beams in my studio, and supports canvases in much the same way as an easel supports a blackboard. It may be seen on the left of plate 20. As an easel it has the advantage of being extremely portable within the studio, and can be easily moved to accommodate changes of sunlight. I have a second, permanent easel which is a sort of long narrow table made from a six-inch plank with a strong support at either end, and a strong crossbar running a few feet above, against which large pictures may be placed. This can be seen to the right of plate 20. On the whole, however, I prefer to work on the floor (plate 18) when painting in an abstract style or when constructing assemblages, as I can walk around the picture and look at it from all points of view.

A palette may be anything you can mix your paints on. The traditional design of the large kidney-shaped palette is an attempt to make a well-balanced working surface which may be held in the hand without undue fatigue, but in fact there is no real reason why a palette need be held in the hand at all. I prefer to mix my colours on a sheet of glass on top of an old box. The flat stone on top of the box is to add weight and thus stability to the support. There is absolutely no need to buy a palette. Even the very expensive ones tend to be overbalanced with large amounts of pigment on them, and they then tire the hands whilst the thumb hole cuts into the base of the thumb. A sheet of glass is much better as a working surface, and may be thrown away when its surface is overloaded with hardened pigment. Any non-absorbent surface will do almost as well, however.

Palette knives are used both for mixing the paint on the palette and for actually laying on the pigment onto the canvas. Here again they are expensive to buy, yet relatively easy to make. A really good small springy palette knife can be made from a filed-down hacksaw blade fixed into a cane handle. Many artists frown on knife painting: they argue that it is not natural (whatever that may mean) to apply paint with a knife instead of a brush, and that the smooth surface of the paint tends to crinkle as it dries. In fact this

ruffling of the paint surface can be very effective, and, as the work of Jackson Pollock shows, some very beautiful pictures have been made out of knife strokes. What was a suitable technique for Turner can hardly be brought into serious question.

Brushes are about the only thing one should not try to economise on. A bad brush is a very bad brush indeed, and, generally speaking, one can evaluate the quality of the brush in terms of its price. A bad brush will lose its shape after a little use, and every time it is applied to the canvas with its hairs loaded with paint it loses its shape and leaves a daub instead of a good clean brush stroke. A good quality brush will keep its shape both in the actual stroke and after continual use.

Brushes come in various sizes, three shapes and only one kind of hair that is any use. The size number you will find written on the brush handle and this refers to the size of the brush head and not to the length of the handle. The shape of the bristles may be flat (sometimes called square), round or filbert, and each shape has a purpose. The flat brush is excellent for applying daubs of paint in an oblong stipple, whereas filbert is useful for applying daubs of paint, and for scumbling in large areas. The round brush is most useful for 'drawing' with paint. The material for a good oil brush is hog-bristle. Any other hair or synthetic bristle is of little practical use (plate 18).

It is possible to paint in oils with a soft brush such as a squirrel or sable, but these are best left for water colour or line and wash, for they do not quite fit the technique of oil painting.

Brushes need to be cleaned very frequently if they are to remain serviceable. They should be rinsed in petrol or turpentine and then washed in warm soapy water. Care must be taken to ensure that all the vestiges of paint at the bottom of the bristle are removed as they tend to rot the bristle and to give a splayed shape to the brush. After being cleaned the brushes should be smoothed into shape and left flat to dry: they should not be kept in jars with their heads up or down. It is a sound practice to keep a special tray for holding brushes, which may be kept covered when they are not actually in use as dust is harmful to them.

Oil paint may be applied to almost any surface, but for

the picture to retain its colour intensity and surface patina the surface must be treated in a special way. The most common surface for oil painting is canvas which has been stretched flat on wooden supports. It is not advisable for the beginner to use stretched canvas, for it is extremely expensive and not so satisfactory as one is led to suppose. Canvas is very easily torn and dented, particularly so when it is stretched drum-tight, and unless it has been well prepared to prevent the oil from actually touching the canvas it will start to rot in patches. The canvas boards which are sold in art shops usually have an insufficient backing of cardboard, and consequently the whole canvas tends to buckle concavely.

By far the best cheap painting surface is prepared hardboard. It has a surface texture similar to that of canvas, though it tends to have an unpleasant 'mechanical' feeling about it which canvas does not have. Hardboard does not require expensive stretching frames, and it is infinitely more durable than canvas.

Wood is a pleasant surface to paint on, particularly with a palette knife, but the surface of wood often has deposits

of resin on the surface which are harmful to oil paint, and it must therefore be prepared with very special care. Also, of course, wood rots and is subject to beetle infestation.

The preparation of a working surface is much the same for almost any material. It must be such as to make the surface water-proof and non-porous by first a glue coating and second a white lead coating. Since it is practical to prepare several surfaces at the same time you should determine the sizes you are likely to require and then make them as rigid as possible by nailing wooden frames onto the back (assuming that you intend to paint on hardboard). The best frames are made by running a firm strip of wood around the perimeter of the board, flush with its edge. If necessary one or two supporting pieces of wood can be run diagonally or vertically across from the middles of two opposite sides. Before nailing the wooden struts down it is advisable to give them a coating of size which will help to make the surface of the back water-proof. When the surface is quite firm it must be given a coat of good size to the back and the front, and then allowed to stand vertically for about a week to dry hard. The next coating should be of white lead

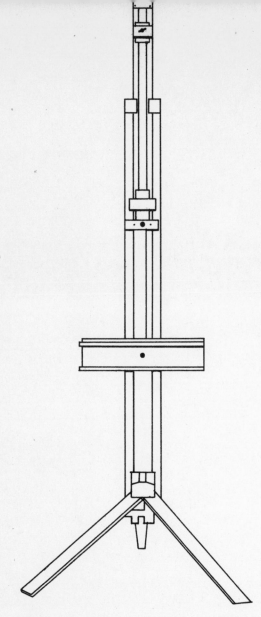

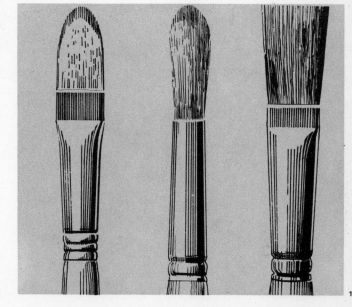

18

which is best purchased in a tin from an art shop, but which can be made by mixing about two thirds of white lead to one third of linseed oil, and then diluting the mixture with turpentine. An excellent primer, which may be applied directly to hardboard, is sold in tins at most art shops. It is expensive, but permits the preparation of a canvas to be completed in a fortnight.

Oil colour, as its name implies, is a powder colour bound with an oil such as walnut, poppy or linseed. Although the common practice is to buy these in tubes already prepared for working, it is much cheaper to purchase the powder colour and mix one's own on the palette as they are required. This last practice demands considerable knowledge of the natures of the respective colours, which knowledge can only be gained by personal experience, so for the first steps in painting at least it is a good idea to buy the prepared oil paints. Large tins of 'Student's Oils' are much more economical than the small tubes of artist's colours.

Oil paint can be applied in a variety of ways ranging from thin transparent stains, obtained by mixing a large amount of thinning medium with a small amount of colour,

to the fat streaks of pure oil paint applied to the canvas directly from the tube. On the whole it is bad practice to paint very thickly, as oil colour, particularly the cheap variety, tends to crack as it dries. The oil colour may be thinned with a variety of oils in much the same way as water colour may be thinned with the addition of water. It may be diluted with oil, varnish or turpentine, but the most commonly used and technically safe is turpentine. In fact there is a limit to which oil colour may be thinned with turpentine, but for all practical purposes it is the best thinner to use.

The composition, nature and properties of oil paint make a fascinating study completely out of the scope of this book. What has to be learned about colour density, drying speeds and the many other considerations which go into the choice of colours for painting is best done through experience. All colours can, in practice, be mixed together, and though some dry more quickly than others, and some change slightly in hue and tone, all colours are, over a period of years, impermanent. The chances of a painting being a 'failure' from lack of experience in material

19 Wall textures from Hampton Court. Reproduced by Gracious Permission of Her Majesty the Queen

19

20

conditions is infinitely less than the chances of its being a 'failure' through other causes.

A common procedure is for an artist to 'varnish' a finished oil painting. This has the direct advantage of enhancing the quality of the picture and of protecting the surface of the oil paint from discolouration, but the disadvantage of turning the picture brown or black because the varnish itself, whatever its quality, will quickly become discoloured. Varnish can be removed at intervals of time and replaced. In fact, this is one of the conservation duties of art galleries. It is quite an experience to see a picture one is very familiar with suddenly returned to its place stripped of its old skin of varnish after some weeks of absence in the 're-varnishing' and restoring departments of the gallery.

Artists often tend to be impatient of the time involved in varnishing, and they do not allow a sufficient interval of time to elapse between the completion of the painting and the final varnishing. The result of this impatience is that the varnish cracks and makes the surface of the picture look very unpleasant. Bad varnishing will completely ruin a painting, and it is almost incredible that certain galleries used to arrange for artists to varnish pictures just before an exhibition, when half of the paintings were scarcely dry from the easel.

We are still far from mastering these technical problems, for the difficulties involved in making sure that a painting will survive for many years are enormous. It would appear that the qualities of paint and paint accessories have degenerated in the past hundred years or so since artists stopped preparing their own materials and began to purchase them from commercial sources. It is, for example, well known that commercially prepared linseed oil is by far inferior to the linseed oil obtained by crushing the seeds. It is not purely a matter of manual dexterity that a painting such as van Eyck's *Arnolfini*, one of the earliest of oil paintings, should still be as fresh now as the day it was painted, whilst many of the pictures of Sickert, done at the beginning of the century, are already faded and spoiled.

An excellent experiment for those who are unaccustomed to painting in oil colours is to paint a small canvas with three or four areas of black and white, so that each area, by virtue of the different methods of application, has a different texture. Plate 22 shows a very thin application of oil and turpentine being washed onto the canvas board. Plate 23 shows the application of an *impasto* of undiluted paint whilst plate 24 shows the finished experiment. The grey of the background has been allowed to 'run' by propping the painting in a vertical position whilst it dried. Simple experiments like this are useful for those who wish to catch the 'feel' of handling oils, but they are not necessary for anyone who is already familiar with oil technique.

Like oil paint, water colour may be applied in thin washes or in loaded bodies of pure pigment, though it cracks even more easily and certainly more quickly than thick oil does and is a medium best thought of in terms of thin washes. For those who prefer to work in thick slabs of colour there is a special paint called gouache, which is an opaque water colour.

The type of paper one uses is of much greater importance than the paints, for it is the paper which, by its absorbent properties, its stiffness and its surface texture, determines the visual-tactile surface of the paint and the eventual survival of the picture. Watercolour painting is not so fraught with technical difficulties as oil painting, so with the right type of paper one is on more or less safe ground. The best paper for drawing and for water painting is of a heavy nature, substantially thick and absorbent. Cheap sheets of cartridge paper are suitable for normal work, whilst rolls of white backing paper which may be bought from decorator's shops are useful for odd doodling as well as for protecting table tops and drawing boards. Its highly absorbent surface makes it very useful for relief printing, though too much water in the paint sometimes causes the colour to spread in the minute paper fibres and this gives a ragged edge to the paint area. All the children's drawings reproduced in this book which have been produced under my tuition have been printed or drawn either on backing paper or on flimsy typing paper. Most beginners do not realise that the majority of papers are only intended to be worked on one side. If you take a sheet of ordinary cartridge paper and hold it at an angle to your eyes so that light rays are reflected at an acute angle from the paper surface you will either see an irregular texture or a regular, mechanical texture. The mechanical texture is the result of the way the

22

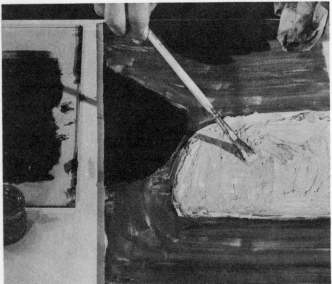

23

24

25

paper has been manufactured, and is not a suitable surface for drawing or painting. If you try a simple shaded drawing on the reverse side of a sheet of cartridge paper you will see how the mechanical grain spoils the appearance of the drawing.

A sketchbook is the most important item of equipment an artist can possess. Sickert, who was a fine actor as well as a great painter, used to speak about his sketchbooks as 'places for private rehearsals', which sums up admirably the place of a sketchbook in the life of an artist. In a sketchbook nothing matters except what one learns and records. What is in the sketchbook will depend on the individual's interest, and how the pages are laid out will depend on his own sensitivity. The best sketchbooks, in my opinion, are the 'wild' ones in which drawing is superimposed upon drawing in the most chaotic way to make the most of available space.

Spirally bound sketchbooks are best for normal use because one can turn the pages over without cracking the binding. The paper quality in all but the most expensive books is usually very poor so it is best to buy a fairly expensive one with good cartridge sheets inside and a stout cardboard back as a rest. The size of the book will vary with requirements. A pocket sketchbook is useful for making odd notes, but quite useless for most sketching purposes. The usual size which art students use is $10'' \times 14''$, which is quite a practical size. Bigger sketchbooks are too heavy to hold for very long, rather clumsy for sketching in a crowd, and in any case the paper inside may be bought much cheaper in separate sheets. Some students scorn a sketchbook and carry around a wooden panel with a number of cartridge sheets held onto it with bulldog clips. This practice does not foster the 'sketch book attitude', for it is only too easy to dispense with 'bad' drawings by detaching the sheet and throwing it away. The essence of a sketchbook is that it should be a record of failure as well as success, so every mark you make in a sketchbook should be preserved.

Practice, which involves experiment, failure, success and constant application, is the only arbiter of materials and methods. Rembrandt is supposed to have drawn a masterpiece with a stick of charred wood snatched from a brazier, and Reynolds is said to have begun his painting career using unprepared sailcloth. It was almost an accident that

27

Senefelder, experimenting with different techniques, discovered the principles upon which lithography is based. Experiment with materials and methods is as important as experiment with basic design: there is no reason why one shouldn't try painting in water colours onto canvas, varnish watercolour prints, scratch designs onto slate or study abstract design by drawing in a layer of salt scattered on a table top (plate 26). So long as one makes an honest attempt to create works of art it matters very little, ultimately, how one sets about it.

In recent months a new type of paint has been put on the market. This is sold under the trade name of Cryla, and is a quick-drying paint with some of the advantages of oil paint. Provided that Cryla is not mixed with the special medium the paint dries fairly hard within half an hour of application. The medium, which is sold with the paints, acts as a thinning agent for the mixing of colours and also retards the drying.

Although Cryla resembles oil colour in many ways, it has a rather unpleasant skin, a defect which can be used to some advantage however, for I have found Cryla particularly useful for experimental work in which I have wanted to obtain a certain crudeness of colour, as for example in *Homage to a Clown*, plate 11. Something of the crudeness disappears when the paint is mixed with the medium, and it is possible to achieve delicate passages of paint where required. *Homage to a Child*, plate 27, was painted in Cryla colour – the areas of bright colour were painted with raw colour, whilst the delicate tones of ochres and browns were painted with the medium added to the mixed colours. One great advantage of the new paint is that it can be used effectively on almost any surface which has first been prepared by a special primer. On the whole Cryla is not so satisfactory to handle as oil paint; one misses the familiar smell and the paintiness of oils, but its quick-drying property gives it a status not of a competitor with oils, but as a useful parallel technique.

The Subject

In principle, anything is a fit subject for the artist, but we have to be quite clear in our minds what we mean by 'subject'. Is the subject of a picture the actual thing depicted – a horse, say – or is it the whole complex of problems with which the artist is wrestling when he sets out to paint? On the face of it the child's drawing of a cowboy and his horse is of much the same subject as Chagall's painting *The Green Donkey* (plate 28), which has a subject which is extremely difficult to describe. It is taken from Russian folklore, and this may be regarded as its real subject, but the 'artistic' subject is Chagall's attempt to reconcile discordant colour elements and to communicate a highly charged emotional atmosphere. It is clear that the real subject of the painting is directly related to the reasons for which it was created.

An artist usually choses his subject (by this I mean the direct pictorial subject such as a horse, a peasant or a cowboy) in terms of the problems with which he is preoccupied. Degas did not choose to paint ballet dancers (plate 29) merely because he liked the sight of pretty girls or because he liked to watch the ballet – his real preoccupation was with nuances of light, fleeting movement, subtle colour and

unfamiliar body postures, all of which were seen to advantage at the ballet and in rehearsal rooms. These were the 'subject' of his paintings and pastels, not 'the ballet'. Art students are given nude figures as subjects not so much because there is anything intrinsically artistic about a nude but because the human body is a most complex relationship of forms – and a student is studying the problems of representing form. Form is his subject, not the nude.

As each pictorial subject brings its own range of problems it doesn't really matter what the beginner chooses to draw or paint. As his awareness of the problems of art deepens, he will instinctively move towards those subjects which help him in his attempts to solve these problems.

One tends to be very conservative in relation to one's subject matter. It is very easy for a painter to become familiar with a subject and because of his success with it to be reluctant to explore new grounds. Painters often like to think of themselves as 'portrait artists', 'landscape painters', 'still life painters' or 'abstract artists', instead of thinking of themselves as 'artists'. It is all well and good for an artist who has found his *métier*, like Rembrandt or Cézanne, to

29

restrict himself to portraiture or landscape painting, but for a student it is downright dangerous to 'specialise', for until he has a great knowledge, 'to specialise' can only mean 'to limit one's field of experience'. A new subject is an adventure, and for this reason alone one should attempt a diversity of subjects to catch something of the creative adventure involved in being an artist.

If you already have a well established repertoire of subjects you are well advised to try to experiment with a subject entirely out of your familiar world of experience. Choose some subject or title – it may be descriptive or nonsensical – and paint two or three pictures which are variations on the theme of your subject or title. The drawings at plates 30, 31 and 32 are three variations on a theme *Angry Cosmic Fragment*. In each case the form and composition of the picture was derived from a study of microphotographs of cellular structures. Each painting is an attempt to create some abstract form which has an integrated structure of its own, a compelling 'presence' and a strong feeling of anger and revolt.

Another way to tackle a painting which is slightly out of

the common run of subject matter is to attempt an illustration of a poem or story with which you are familiar. Literary themes are not very much in vogue nowadays, but this is no reason why one should not experiment freely with the problems involved in 'illustrative painting'.

There are several ways of approaching a literary theme, but the two main ways consist either of making a descriptive comment or of creating a visual parallel to something which was originally literary. All illustration falls within the first category, for the artist chooses some incident in a story or poem and describes it in visual terms. The sculptural assemblage *Homage to Kafka* (plate 34) falls within the second category, for although it does not illustrate any particular passage from Kafka's Castle, it re-creates in visual terms the hero's confusion and inertia in his bewildering search for the elusive Klamm. The strange little figure has none of the epic stature of the usual hero of a novel, and the background on which it is placed evokes directly the unreal mechanistic world which mocked Kafka's hero in his attempts to enter The Castle.

Most paintings of biblical scenes are purely illustrative,

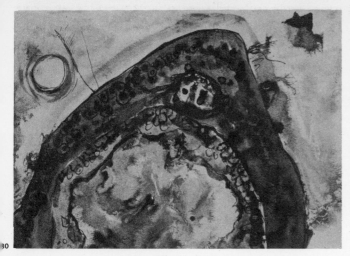

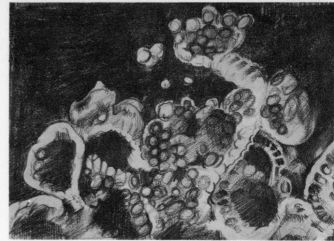

29 Degas, 'Rehearsal of a Ballet on the Stage'. Camondo Collection, Louvre, Paris © S.P.A.D.E.M. Paris, 1965

30-

32 Fred Gettings, 'Variations on a theme "Angry Cosmic Fragment"' Author's collection

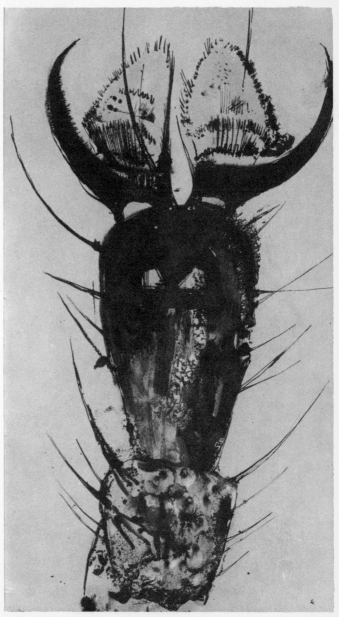

being direct interpretations of a 'literary' theme, but occasionally, as in the work of Stanley Spencer, who often painted biblical scenes in a contemporary setting, the artist is able to create a visual parallel and thereby avoid being purely descriptive.

The picture on plate 35 is an attempt to express in pictorial terms a passage from T. S. Eliot's *Four Quartets*. The illustration had to suggest the wheeling cosmos and the movement of the atom, both movement and rest, the feeling of continual creation and continual destruction.

If such flights of literary fancy do not excite you, it may be more advisable to attempt one or two subjects from the world of visual experience, such as a landscape, a still life or a portrait.

Almost everyone will at some time or another attempt a landscape painting. An artist can go to a landscape to solve practically any problem. He might, like Monet, be exploring light, or like Cézanne, investigating structure: he might wish to translate the moods of nature into paint, like Constable, or to penetrate the essential force of nature like Turner; but whatever his search he will find it in a landscape.

33

34

Popular as landscape painting may be, however, it is usually the most badly painted of all subjects because the problems involved are so immense and so often poorly understood. Anyone who has visited exhibitions of landscape paintings will have learned that a good landscape painting is rare, and a bad one (usually looking rather like a withered lettuce salad) is all too common.

The chief thing to remember when faced with painting a landscape is to be quite clear in your mind what you are wanting to paint or draw. Is it the natural rhythm of organic forms, or is it the pervading light which interests you in a particular view? Do you want to produce a topographical record of a spot or are you more interested in catching the mood of what you see? Any attempt to paint directly from nature without a clear aim will be singularly unproductive.

Paradoxically enough, one of the most satisfactory ways of learning about landscape painting is indoors – in art galleries. After your own attempts to grapple with a problem of painting an outdoor scene, you will learn a great deal from examining the works of one or two of the great masters to see how they have approached problems similar

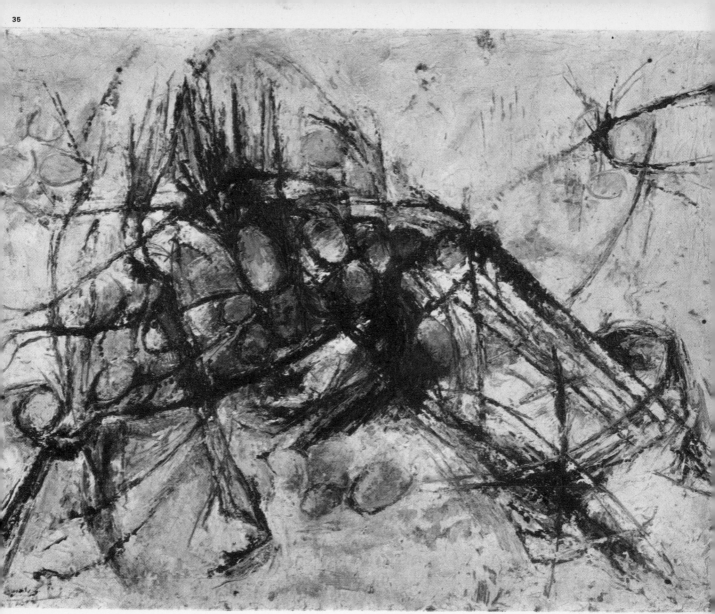

to the ones with which you yourself were faced. You might find in a gallery some picture which inspires you to paint a similar one: you may be impressed by John Constable's *Hadleigh Castle* (plate 33) and decide to tackle a picture of a rain-swept landscape yourself. Your first step should be to make a detailed examination of the painting itself in order to make quite sure how the particular effects you admire have been achieved. In *Hadleigh Castle* one first perceives the masterly restraint of colour which creates a feeling of 'grey depression', then one observes how the treatment of texture in the sky has been carried into the castle and foreground so as to convey the atmosphere so peculiar to rainy days. Constable has a peculiar technique of leaving flecks of white paint shining out from the dark tones, and in this picture they work very well in suggesting the glistening of reflected light on the drenched surfaces. In addition, the thick *impasto* applications of paint (on the walls of the castle most noticeably), reflect the light from the gallery and contribute towards the impression of wet surfaces.

Once you have seen how a particular technique has been employed to obtain a particular result you will be in a much

better position to attempt a similar subject yourself. Your next undertaking must be to try to relate Constable's observations to nature, what you have seen in the picture to what you see in actual fact. You must 'rehearse' the scene as dispassionately as possible. First of all you must try to register the 'mood' of the rain-swept scene by taking a 'mental snapshot' of the broad essentials by looking at the scene with half-closed eyes or without focusing on any one thing. When you have registered the general impression, and have, perhaps, made one or two broad colour sketches of the scene before you, you can begin particular observations. You must make a note of how the clouds' movement affects the change of light, and how this in its turn affects the colour, how the rain falls, and how its movement can best be described or suggested in terms of paint. In this connection you see that in *Hadleigh Castle* Constable has not resorted to the method of 'painting in' drops of rain with white slashes of paint as a lesser artist might have done, yet for some reason one is very much aware of rain being carried on the gusts of wind. This impression is probably a result of the broad handling of the paint which unites the

sky and foreground behind a 'film of texture', and suggests an aqueous atmosphere of rain and wind which creates a film between the observer and the landscape.

Once you have tried to see nature through a painter's eyes by translating every effect into paint, and once you have accumulated a number of notes and sketches, you will be in a position to build up a painting of the outdoor scene in your studio. This is much more difficult than one might suppose: it is not easy to catch the feeling of spontaneity so essential to the landscape art when one is not working 'from life'. The sketches of Constable are particularly famous because in many cases, before doing a 'finished studio painting' for exhibition, he would make a rapid sketch of exactly the same subject, and nowadays the fresh spontaneity of these preparatory sketches are admired far above the somewhat laboured, though technically admirable, exhibition pieces. Try first to sacrifice everything towards capturing this spontaneity – not because there is any particular virtue in spontaneity in itself, but because nature is alive, and an over-worked painting is often dead.

When your picture is complete you can return to the gallery and examine once more the painting which originally inspired you to face the elements. You will be very surprised to find how your understanding and appreciation of the picture has changed. Your own attempts will have made you much more appreciative of how the artist came to terms with nature: instead of merely seeing paint on a canvas you will see the mind of the artist at work – and this is the first step towards true appreciation.

If you find yourself at all interested in landscape painting you might set yourself the task of making a close study of three different landscape artists and attempt to learn how their particular interests contribute to the style of their works. Perhaps you might interest yourself in Cézanne and study his underlying sense of structure, or in Palmer and study his mystic depth, or in Ruisdael and study his grasp of light and space. The greatest of all nature painters, William Turner, is worth a lifetime of study. There is in Turner a little of Cézanne, Palmer and Ruisdael – and every landscape artist who came after him. The diversity of Turner's works is the most astonishing thing, and little is more rewarding than a close study of all the paintings

collected together in the Tate Gallery.

Of course, as we have already seen, because you are faced with a landscape it does not necessarily mean that you have to interpret it in realistic terms. You may work along the lines of the painting in plate 36, in which your interest in the abstract pattern of trees against a background of snow results in a picture which is highly decorative and almost abstract. You may, on the other hand, be even more abstract and produce a work something like the one by Trewin Copplestone. In *Cleft Landscape* (plate 38), he attempts to symbolise the life force. The two white ovals buried in the earth represent two huge wombs, the source of natural life. The immense cleft right into the earth resembles a volcanic vent from which the life force flows into the world. The black 'smoke' on the surface of the earth suggests the destructive, disintegrating action of the wind, which is also instrumental in propagating life by carrying the seeds of flowers and trees (the black spots in the air) and depositing them on the earth. The orange, ochres and reds of the earth suggest the quickening properties of soil, whilst the black smoke caught in the wind's movement represents death. Between the pure white of the womb-like shapes and the black winds of destruction is the thin film of top soil from which life arises in its preordained rhythm, and the stratification of this top soil suggests the cyclic changes of which life is the manifestation.

A still life, that is to say any arrangement of objects, is at first glance a simpler task. Unlike a landscape it will keep still – particularly if the light is artificial. You will have an excellent opportunity to study the abstract patterns and the tonal qualities which exist as a result of the juxtaposition of the objects before you. Accurate observation and accurate draughtsmanship are necessary, a sense of space and a sense of balance, but here again, you must establish precisely what qualities in the still life interest you most. Is it the pattern of bottles, or is it the delicate colouring on the fishes' scales which have caught your attention? In still life painting, as in every other form of painting, one must question oneself in order to establish an intention.

Portraiture cannot be approached with quite the same detachment as landscape painting, for we react in a very

38

36 'Landscape with Snow', by Edwin Thubron, aged 16, Leeds College of
    Art. Reproduced by courtesy of the Sunday Mirror

37 Samuel Palmer, 'Moonlight – a landscape with Sheep'. Ashmolean
    Museum, Oxford

38 Trewin Copplestone, 'Cleft Landscape'. Private Collection

39

different way to a face than to a tree. Although the basic problems of portraiture are much the same as in any other kind of object drawing (that is to say, problems of structure, light, composition, form and so on), sufficient objectivity is needed to make a portrait not merely a good drawing or painting, but a good 'likeness'. A likeness may be a good drawing, but it may also be a bad drawing, whereas a good drawing must, almost by definition, be a likeness. Because of this one must resign oneself to making good drawings rather than good likenesses. Other than this, very little practical advice can be offered about portraiture. The way to learn is to attempt as best you can one or two drawings of people you know and then turn to the great portrait painters of the past and examine their methods. Holbein, Rembrandt and Dürer, to mention only three masters, may be studied with profit for a whole lifetime. When you become aware of a specific problem – it may be how to draw an eye so that it looks as though it actually fits into the socket in the skull, or it may be how to relate the head of your sitter to his neck – go to the drawings of these masters and see how they have solved the problem.

A common difficulty for all portrait painters is how to suggest the age of their sitters with reasonable accuracy in preliminary drawings. As one must draw in line there is a tendency for a portrait drawing to look much older than it should. A line drawn round the eye, for example (and this is the only way to indicate the eye with a pencil) has the same effect as a line drawn in grease paint around an actor's eye: it makes him look older. This problem becomes acute when one attempts to draw a child.

As an exercise in portraiture, try drawing two pictures of someone you know with different aims in mind. Try in one picture to catch the force of the sitter's personality and in the other to make a record of the sitter's physical likeness. You will be astonished to see how two different styles of drawing emerge from these two attempts, particularly if you use different techniques, as with the two examples reproduced here. The self-portrait by twelve-year-old Ian Morton (plate 40) was drawn with a brush, whereas the portrait at plate 41 was executed first in pencil with a rubbing of red conté crayon, and then touched up with nervous flicks of Indian ink. Once you

41

40

have done these two different portraits, your next problem
will be to make an attempt to incorporate these two
aspects of the sitter, the inner personality and the outer
personality, in one portrait. The ability to do this is the
mark of the proficient artist, so do not become too
discouraged if you do not succeed at first.

In practice the best way to study every subject is first to
make an honest attempt to draw and paint from direct
observation, and then to examine the work of masters who
have excelled in the field. Do not be afraid to copy the
methods used by reputable artists provided you learn by
so doing, for this was the basis of the apprenticeship
system in art studios until two hundred years ago. All
works of art have a debt, acknowledged or otherwise, to
the works of art which preceded them. Mere copying is an
anathema; *intelligent* copying is half the secret of art.

39 Breughel, 'The Artist with a Connoisseur' (detail). Albertina, Vienna

40 'Portrait' by Ian Morton, aged 12, Cray Valley Technical School, Kent.
Reproduced by courtesy of the Sunday Mirror

41 Fred Gettings, 'Portrait'. Author's collection

Basic Design

42

In recent years, as a result of the teaching methods of such artists as Klee, Gropius and Malevich, an entirely new approach to art teaching has been initiated in this country. The old traditional form of teaching art consisted of sitting a student before a model or a still life in the hope that in his struggle to represent form he would learn how to draw. In addition to this he was taught 'Composition' in which he learned to arrange colours, patterns, forms and symbols onto a canvas or sheet of paper so that he would develop a sense of design. The only thing wrong with this method of teaching was that it produced artists 'in a vacuum'. When the student finally left art school he found that he had mastered to a more or less proficient degree a series of techniques and methods and had adopted a series of attitudes towards art which bore no relationship to either the problems of design posed by modern industry or the search being made by the leading painters and draughtsmen of today. As a result of this the student had to spend several years forgetting what he had learned at art school in order to fit himself into the contemporary social structure. Those students who appreciated the problems involved and did make some attempt to free themselves of the limitations of art school discipline were trammeled by examination requirements, and up to a few years ago it was no uncommon thing for a promising student of art to fail his examinations because his view of what was 'art' did not correspond to the views held by examination boards.

Several schools of art are now practising a new and more enlightened method of teaching which has not quite superseded the traditional academic teaching, but in many cases runs parallel to it. This new method of teaching is sometimes called 'Basic Design Theory', and in essence it consists of presenting the student with a series of graphic problems which he must attempt to solve. This approach to art permits a student to develop an attitude of enquiry towards design in particular and art in general, an attitude which was so often absent in students who were a product of the old method of teaching. The chief aim of Basic Design courses is not to teach a student how to pass examinations, or even how to produce good art work, but how to foster a new attitude to art and to teach him a new language by which he may interpret his understanding of the world.

More than any other art discipline, Basic Design demands a close relationship between student and teacher, for it is not a series of disciplines which is being taught, but a whole complex of attitudes to art and life. Nevertheless, provided that the student is able to see that in basic design the problem with which he is faced is more important than the solution to that problem, he will be able to experiment along certain lines without a teacher.

One way of coming to grips with the problems of basic design is to pose yourself several graphic problems of an elementary nature. Cut up a sheet of black paper into small squares and start arranging them on sheets of white card. As you experiment you will see that as one piece of black paper has been placed against its white background a relationship is established between the black and white surfaces, and as soon as a second black square is placed next to it the first relationship is destroyed and quite a new one is formed. Every addition of a black square changes the relationship between all the others and creates a new design. It is this continual destruction and re-creation which is the basis of the art process, and for this reason it must be studied as deeply as possible.

Perhaps you would like to set yourself a problem in this connection. Arrange three rows of seven black squares onto a sheet of white paper to make an interesting structural design like the one in plate 43. When you have done this to your satisfaction, you can then attempt to build up a new structure over the existing one and establish a new formal relationship on the paper (plates 44 and 45). Each black square must be carefully considered in relationship to the whole before it is allowed to remain and before the next one is brought for consideration.

At this point you may have observed that your design is very linear, that you have laid a sort of pathway of squares in which there is no circular movement at all. Your problem is now to introduce a circular motion into this same design to give it visual 'life' and yet at the same time to preserve the formal pattern of the whole design (plate 46). It would be a good idea to experiment on a separate sheet with the sorts of rhythms which can be obtained with the black squares. Put the drawing upon which you are working aside and take up a new sheet of card upon which you build a

44

5

46

7

48

A

C

D

49

B

E

50 Trewin Copplestone, 'Summer Landscape'. Artist's collection

design carefully avoiding any 'linear stepping stones' and introduce a greater freedom of movement than you achieved in the previous design. You might experiment something along the lines of the two designs on plate 48, in which the movement is brisk, or along the lines of plate 47 in which the movement is subdued and formal, but once you have seen how the black squares may be used to create a rhythmic movement you should turn once more to your first design and face the problem of introducing a circular movement into the design without ruining its basic underlying structure.

In the above series of experiments we have been struggling with the nature of relationships. A black square is, from a graphic point of view, nothing but a dot in one dimension. When it is placed within the white square it establishes a relationship with its area and its sides and is changed from a point to a tension because it exerts a force within the picture area. When two or a few more black squares are placed together they form accumulated tensions, but when they are placed in a definite order (like 'stepping stones') they lose their individuality and turn into a line with force and direction. A line built out of separate sheets of black squares

is much more lively in appearance than a single strip of black paper, but it does not have the same strength of direction. You can confirm this experimentally by placing a line or a series of lines built out of long black strips into a design with some static elements such as large black squares and then replacing the strips with an equivalent length of small black squares. You should try to experiment in this way so as to learn for yourself something about the different formal natures of points, lines and masses.

Now take a large sheet of paper or card, a small brush and some indian ink and try to find a graphic solution to the following problems. Four curvilinear lines are to be placed in a relationship to each other without actually touching (Fig. A plate 49). Four curvilinear lines are to be related by four other curvilinear lines of a different texture (Fig. B plate 49). A series of small circles are to be built around a central circle to establish a free relationship of forms (Fig. C plate 49). A strong vertical line is cut in half by a vortex stream (Fig. D plate 49). A circular shape of an irregular nature is to be contained within three lines (Fig. E plate 49). Your own solutions to these five problems

51-55 Progression in basic design

need not resemble in any way the solutions given as examples in the illustrations, nor should you worry about how 'aesthetic' your solutions look.

Your next problem springs from the above exercise, for you have to relate at least three out of your five motifs into one design. If you look closely at Copplestone's *Summer Landscape* (plate 50) you will discover that at least four motifs from the illustrations on page 32 have been incorporated into a single painting. Observe particularly the difference between the graphic approach to these motifs and the painterly approach.

Now take another large sheet of paper and in the left hand corner do a small black and white design from two very simple motifs. Select one of these motifs and on the right of the design draw a simplified version of it. Now do several variations on this visual theme, and see what sort of shape you end up with. Your aim should be continually to refine and simplify the shape or to make it more and more complex, but whichever you do, each step should be evident in the series of variations. You could quite easily follow the thought processes in the series of illustrations from plate 55.

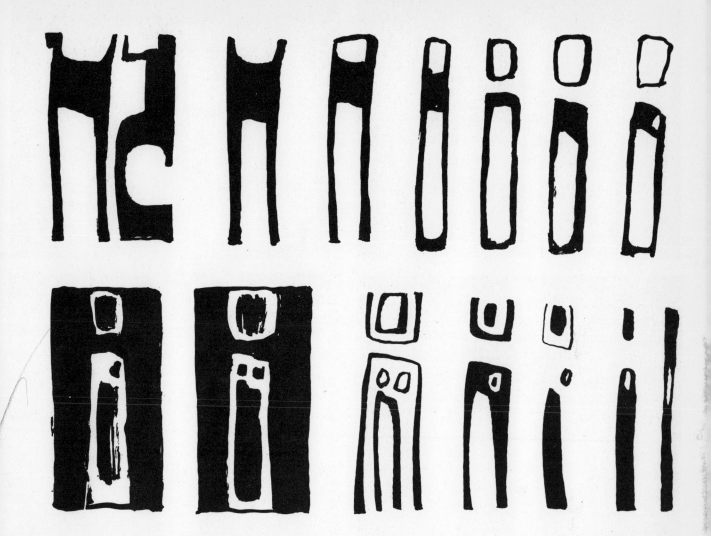

The first drawing is an attempt to create an 'ambiguous image' in which the shapes may be looked at as either black shapes imposed on white or white shapes imposed on black. It is the left hand one of these two shapes which is chosen for graphic development, and in the first instance the shape is simplified by changing the top left hand projection and making the whole shape a little more symmetrical. In the next variation the top projections are joined so that the black form now contains a white shape, and the next form follows much the same lines in that the bottom is joined to change the projections into a contained white space. Now the two containing shapes are separated into two, and what set out as a flat black image has now changed into two white areas bordered by black lines. The next development is towards turning the lower black line once more into a shape by thickening it and adding weight to its top. In the next drawing part of this black shape is made a little more complicated by adding a third white space at the top.

Take the motif which you drew last in this series of developments and reverse its image by painting in the white areas black and the black areas white. You now have another theme upon which you can create visual variations. The bottom row of plate 55 represents an attempt to suggest a series of variations on a reversed image. The second drawing differs from the first by the addition of a second black shape, but this at once turns the drawing into a figure with the top shape a head, the bottom shape its body and the two black spots its breasts. In the next variation this 'Presence' is retained, but the black surround is dispensed with, and once more we have an arrangement of lines which create an ambiguous image. The development on this is to reverse the image again so that black becomes white. This simplifies the shape and also changes the representative nature of the figure so that the body is changed into legs and the head is considerably diminished and contained within the upraised arms. The next variation is the result of an attempt to destroy the figure by once more changing black to white. The separate circle of black is next incorporated into a very simple shape and the final variation reduced to two separate shapes and then to one single vertical form with a hole in its middle.

This type of approach to basic design is very productive in that it liberates the mind from the conventional attitude to art, and yet ties it down to providing a series of practical problems and solutions in terms of abstract form. Each solution is in itself capable of infinite development, and it will be a rewarding exercise to take any one of the designs evolved on your sheet of thematic variations and turn it into an abstract painting. *Blue Abstract* on plate 56 contains within it the theme of plate 55. The head of the figure has been translated into a thin wash of paint surrounded by a blue halo, and the body is a sheet of sacking upon which has been built a solid slab of paint scumbled with light blue.

Basic design implies that one is going to fill a great number of sheets of paper with visual ideas. One might, for example, experiment along the lines of the paintings (plates 58 to 60), working out the variations which can be made with three simple areas of white against a black background with sheets of paper and a brush loaded with black paint instead of with oil paint (the medium in which the *Landscape* variations are painted). To make only twenty or thirty such variations entails a great consumption of paper, so one could resort to newspaper as a base. The texture of the columns of print and photographs often gives rise to 'happy accidents' of design, and are certainly instrumental in posing additional problems in that the typographic texture of the sheet on which you are working must be taken into account each time you try a variation on a given theme. Franz Kline, the American painter, used to explore graphically in a telephone book, trying out different design possibilities in black and white, using one page at a time. He said that he could go right through a whole volume of the telephone directory in one night.

Besides being a source of cheap paper, newsprint often contains photographs with exciting graphic and plastic potential. The camera has been of great value to many great artists. Degas and Sickert used photographs in their exploration of compositional possibilities, and both of them grew fond of the type of composition in which part of a figure was cut off in an unexpected way, leaving a patterned shape related to the edge of the photograph. Ben Shahn has painted several very fine pictures from snap shots of people in positions which appear to be unnatural

58

58 Fred Gettings, 'Abstract One'. Collection of Trewin Copplestone

59 Fred Gettings, 'Abstract Two'. Private collection

60 Fred Gettings, 'Abstract Three'. Author's collection

61 Basic design experiment with coins

59

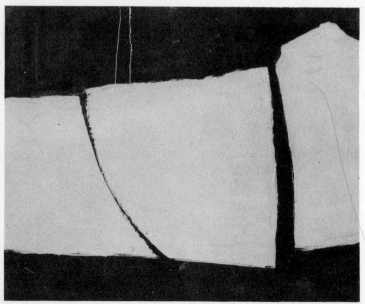

62

63

because they are isolated in movement and time. Many painters have been influenced by sequence photographs in which a series of swift actions are preserved on one exposure. All these developments are a result of the experimental attitude to art which is so far removed from that of the commercial painter who will produce a portrait from a photograph in only a few days. To sum up, I would say that to make an accurate copy of a photograph once or twice may be an interesting discipline but constant repetition of this discipline would lead nowhere. If, however, one were to approach the use of photography from a different point of view, like Degas, Sickert or Shahn, it could be extremely instructive.

Take the photograph of cricketers at plate 62 for example. One might set oneself the task of rearranging all the major figures into a new and more satisfactory composition. To do this one could either cut out the figures or trace them. This is more difficult than one would think as the relationship which exists in the photograph in its present form depends largely on the presence of the cricket ball, which creates a psychological unity in the composition

because each player is orientated towards it. In addition to this the simple structure of the composition would be very difficult to improve on as it is so simple and compact. The two vertical lines formed by the umpire and the bowler on the left and the two batsmen on the right, supporting a horizontal line formed by the four fielders is an almost classic composition in its simplicity. Any attempt to disturb it in its present unified form and then re-compose it will lead to enormous difficulties.

A much simpler exercise would be to try and fit the players into quite different picture areas without disturbing their relationship to each other. The best way of doing this will be to place a sheet of tracing paper over the photograph and trace the limits of the composition over the top, indicating the positions of the figures in sketchy outlines so that you will have a record of the new composition. If you have several photographs from one newspaper you might rearrange them by cutting them out and sticking them onto a sheet of paper.

You might like to choose one aspect of the photograph which interests you and try to isolate it in a drawing.

67 James Thorn, 'Pit Head', sketch. Author's collection
69 James Thorn, 'Pit Head' Author's collection

68

It could be the swerving movement of the bowler in relation to the umpire, or it could be the intentness of a fielder: it may be the pattern created by the batsmen which interests you most of all because you observe that the identity of each figure is merged into a group which forms an interesting shape.

There is almost no end to the experiments one can conduct in the field of basic design, and, provided one is able to remember that it is the search which is important and not what is found, such experiments can only have beneficial results. The purpose behind a basic design course makes itself apparent only very slowly through a student's work. The study of abstract relationships in terms of line, masses and forms gradually takes hold of the mind and begins to change one's awareness of the world. The sign that one is working along the right lines is that one's vision and understanding of the world changes: one becomes aware of more and one sees the outside world from quite a different point of view. One learns, for example, to 'rehearse' the scene before one – whether in a sketchbook or in one's mind – to examine its pictorial possibilities in terms of colour,

composition, distribution of light and shade, and all the abstract relationships of form.

This constant evaluation of the world gradually shows through one's art form as a personal style. What began as a study of abstract relationships changes one's view of life and this new attitude is, in its turn, reflected in one's work. The two sketches at plates 67 and 69 were made by the same student with an interval of just over eighteen months between them during which time he had been studying basic design. Plate 69, although quite obviously executed with more care than plate 67, reflects quite a different attitude. The student, in the intervening months, has obviously learned a great deal about abstract relationships of form, pattern and structure, and this shines through his work in a most impressive way.

Line

Line is in one sense the simplest and in another sense the most complex tool of the artist. It is the simplest tool because it is so easily made – the meeting of graphite with paper – and because it is used instinctively as a medium of expression from our earliest childhood. It is the most complex tool because it is a measure of the artist's sensitivity, technical ability and imagination. How an artist uses line is a measure of his creative depth. As Ingres, the greatest of French draughtsmen, said, 'It takes over thirty years to learn to draw,' and then added, 'but only three days to learn to paint.'

'Nature', said William Blake, 'has no line – but Imagination has.' Line is a convention by which means the aims of the artist are made clear. By this I do not mean merely that there is no line in nature, that the 'outline' of an apple is in reality an illusion made by disappearing planes meeting a background tone; I mean that line is so fundamental to expression and so intimately bound up with the psyche of the artist that it is possible to discover the quality of an artist simply by examining the quality of his line. Imagination has a line, and each of us has a unique imagination.

In the drawing on plate 70 we have an example of a very simple drawing which is the direct outward expression of an inner experience. The drawing was done by a young woman who was suffering from a severe attack of bronchitis. She did the drawing in a state of semi-coma whilst desperately fighting for breath in an oxygen tent. We can only understand this drawing by relating it to the circumstance under which it was produced; it is simply a drawing of a pair of lungs connected by a bronchial tube to a gasping mouth. Every other element – the simple form of the head, the simple sack of the body – has been completely subordinated to the aim of expressing the agonising fight for breath. The line itself is line at its most elemental – it is direct, without any stylistic gimmicks, and it is serving a purpose with the maximum economy. If we compare this simple drawing with the one by Rembrandt on plate 71 we shall see how line may be used for entirely different purposes. The rich quality of line has a threefold aim of describing the voluminous forms of the solid body, of expressing the movement and vitality of the posture and of conveying a sense of weighty balance. This highly

70 Bronchial drawing. Author's collection

71 Rembrandt, 'Standing Woman'. British Museum, London

72 Giovanni Bellini, 'Turkish Janissary'. British Museum, London

73 Brockhurst, 'Standing Woman', etching. Author's collection

74

sophisticated and competent drawing marks the other extreme to which line may be put. It is quite clear from this comparison that lines are more than 'outlines', that they have a value independent of the thing they represent.

A line has a vitality or force of its own. A good artist, simply by varying the strength of his line, can give it a vitality which has the effect not merely of demarcating the boundaries, but also of suggesting the nature of the space enclosed. This can be seen from the line drawing by Picasso of a centaur carrying off a woman (plate 75). Although the line is little more than 'outline', it has quite a different quality from the drawing on plate 74, and somehow Picasso has given the group a sense of weight and solidity. One can feel the swell of the centaur's belly in the first drawing just as much as in the second one which has much 'shading' to emphasise the form.

A most useful and instructive exercise is to attempt to draw a simple form, like a ball, using only its outline to express the nature of its form. A very sensitive line is required to differentiate between a ball and a mere circle. There are no simple tricks or gimmicks to make this fundamental exercise easy: the only way it can be done is by feeling the form of the ball in one's mind and then

projecting it onto the paper. One must realise it as a *solid*, not merely as a 'round' object. If sufficient concentration is used in trying to visualise this solidity before pencil is put to paper the task will not be found impossible.

A line may be regarded as a record of force. It has movement, direction and strength, and each type of line has a quite unique and distinctive feeling about it. A line is almost a living thing. Paul Klee even described one type of drawing exercise as 'taking a line for a walk', as if line were a living creature which had to be guided along under control.

Before we ourselves experiment with taking a line for a walk it will be as well for us to look closely at some of the different types of line we may use. Because a line is a record of force it always has some effect on us – 'All the world knows that even a single line can arouse emotions', said Mondrian. At least a smattering of the language of line must be learned before any real progress in drawing can be made.

The different qualities of line on plate 76 are worth close attention.

The first two lines (A and B) are drawn with an ordinary fine pen. The lines are of equal thickness throughout, and

it is the course of the line which gives the particular 'feeling'. Line B is much more alive because of its erratic course.

Line C was made by varying the pressure of the pen nib as the line was being drawn. This adds a vitality to the line itself, and although the course of the line is much the same as A it is infinitely more lively.

With line D we move away from 'pure line', for it really consists of two lines which run together, continually criss-crossing each other. This is a much slower line, and although again its course is much the same as A, it does not feel quite as alive. It is a turgid line because the eye is being slowed down by its unevenness, just as a sliding object is slowed down on an uneven runway.

Line E is an altogether different kind of line. It is really made up of a vibrating line which is travelling in a certain direction. It is the kind of line which a young child will draw when it has passed the stage of circular scribbling, and some psychologists suggest that the muscular rhythm behind the line is related to the pulse rhythm and thus to the blood flow. Certainly it is a very powerful line. So is line F which has a strong sense of direction and a fine thrusting richness about it. Line G incorporates a massive strength with richness of texture: it is a line which is almost an area with

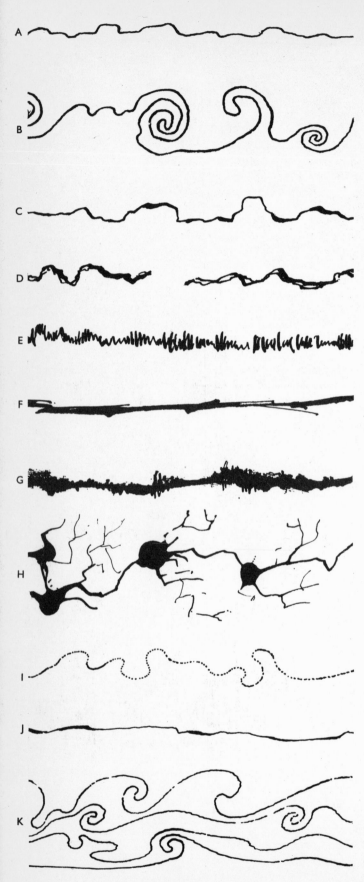

a distinctive shape of its own. It was made by scribbling zig-zag over a line rather like F, and this created an interplay of linear forces which results in a tension between the lines. This interplay interests the eye in much the same way as a polyphony interests the ears.

With line H we come to an 'invented' line, which closely resembles the patterns made by frost on windows. Drawing such lines can be great fun: they are made by putting a small blob of ink on the paper and then tracing fine hair-like lines out of the blob in different directions until the ink is used up. The lines emerge from the blob rather like the roots emerging from the seed, and the whole pattern of lines certainly has an 'organic' feeling about it. Wonderful effects can be obtained by 'smudging' the line with the finger tip as the drawing proceeds (see the section on texture on page 93).

The feeling of the line can be changed a great deal by changing the way in which it is drawn. Line I has been varied by alternating the line with a series of dots. This has the effect of adding a feeling of delicacy. Line J is extremely nervous and sensitive. It was made by dragging the flat edge of the pen along the paper with different pressures on the nib. The blurred effect along the side of the line adds a certain richness of quality to it.

Line K shows how a rich movement can be created by juxtaposing lines of type B. The moving patterns closely resemble the flow of water eddies which so fascinated Leonardo da Vinci. It is quite impossible for the eye to look at one point in such a combination of lines, for it is caught in the swirling movement and travels backwards and forwards in the 'current'.

It is quite impossible to describe the different sense of movement, direction and strength which all the various kinds of line can create in our minds. The only way we can begin to see something of the real significance of line is to fill sheets of paper with as many different kinds of line as possible, all created in as many different ways as possible, so that one can learn something about their qualities. The mastery of line must be compared to the mastery of the scales in music – it is the very basis of art, and one can never exhaust its possibilities.

Drawing from life is one of the most profitable and

76

enjoyable ways of learning about line and its possibilities. The chief difficulty is that one tends to forget one's aim in doing the sketching. You might start out by drawing some trees or some cows in a field or a busy street scene in order to discover the different types of line which are best suited to the subject, but you may be tempted to forget that you are trying to learn about line and become engrossed in 'making a picture' of a tree, a cow or a street scene. You must try to remember that it does not matter what sort of a mess you make so long as you learn something.

Besides drawing from life there are several other ways of experimenting with line. You can either experiment with abstract pictures or with realistic pictures, for you will learn much the same thing from both.

An interesting way of making abstract pictures from line is to draw round some simple object, like a pair of scissors, a fork, a matchbox or a penny. This method usually gives a very sure and certain line, which is a little insensitive and wiry. The problem is to draw round the objects in such a way as to avoid the stiffness of a pure outline (for example, by applying different pressures to the pencil whilst tracing) and to give as much linear variety as one can, by breaking the line at various points, and by adding a texture later on. Plate 78 is a drawing done by a twelve-year-old boy. He drew in ink around the end of a knife blade placed on the paper in different positions, and then afterwards slightly smudged the lines by lightly touching them with his wetted finger tip. He then enriched the texture by adding dots and short lines where he felt they were required. The shapes made by the knife blade have a sufficient similarity to give the picture an intrinsic unity, whilst the inventiveness of placing and the variety of the actual line gives sufficient variety to avoid monotony. The intentional mistakes in the tracing, and the application of texture were only satisfactory after several attempts had been made.

Another interesting way of learning about line is to do several drawings of the same subject in as many different linear styles as possible. As our aim is to learn about line there can be no harm in copying a photograph as a basis for our exercise. We could make a tracing of a simple picture and make several light copies of it in pencil and then proceed to our linear exercise by drawing over in black

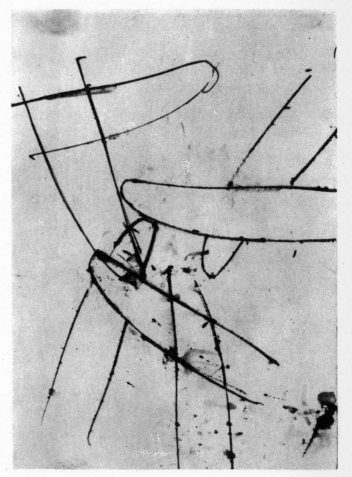

78

79

79 Photograph of footballers by courtesy of The Oxford Mail

83

89 Fred Gettings, illustrations to 'British Trees and Shrubs'. Reproduced by courtesy of the publishers, Ward Lock Ltd

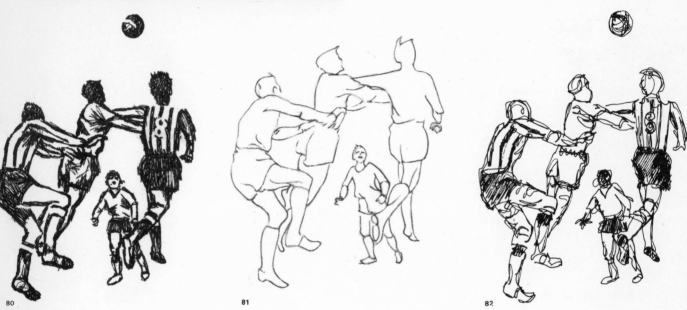

80

81

82

ink. If, for example, we take a photograph of a footballer from a local newspaper, we can make copies in the various linear styles shown at plates 80-82. Each of these drawings can teach us a little about line, and each is pleasant in terms of its own characteristics.

Of course, one should not confine one's experiments to a pen or a pencil. A brush has quite a different range of linear possibilities which one can exploit to great effect. Many of Rembrandt's brush drawings are worth close study, but the greatest exponents of brush work are the Chinese, and one can do no better than examine their calligraphic works to learn something of the use to which the 'wet line' can be put.

Now that we have examined a few of the different properties of line we are in a much better position to start using lines to make pictures. Whether we want to draw 'realistic' pictures, abstract ones or semi-realistic ones like children, the principle is the same – the quality of line must reflect the 'feeling' of the drawing.

Let us take a look at four different ways of drawing, and see how it is possible to use line in an intelligent way.

If we set out to do a drawing of some real object, like a tree, for example, the problem will be to use line in order to describe that particular tree, to bring out its beauty and to create in terms of line a synthesis of its nature.

The best way of beginning such a project is, of course, to actually look at trees – not merely at the tree you have chosen to draw but at as many other types as possible. In this way you can ask yourself 'what makes the particular tree I have chosen to draw different from all others?' If you have chosen to draw an oak tree you will observe that the trunk is generally heavier than that of an elm, that its branches tend to be more gnarled and that the texture of its leaves is quite different. The particular oak tree you have chosen may spread itself out along the ground rather than growing straight up: it may even trail one or two of its branches along the ground. All these characteristics must be taken into account before you actually start to draw.

You will have to reflect on how best to suggest the leaves of the tree, how to catch their 'texture' as a whole, because it is quite impossible to draw each and every leaf. You will have to watch how the leaves group themselves around the

83 84 85

86 87 88 89

main branches, and how this affects the silhouette of the tree (some leaves tend to hang down, others to thrust upwards, whilst others mass in large round clumps). The trees (plates 83-89) were drawn with a special interest in the differences of leaf texture and massing.

If the leaves of the tree are spiky, then the little pen flicks which describe the foliage must be spiky, but if the leaves are tendril-like, then your pen marks must catch their individual rhythmic curves. The overall shape of the tree is very important to your drawing. Does the tree show in general a lot of trunk, and if so what is its general proportion to the leaf clusters? Is the pattern of the tree almost circular, like the sycamore, or is it squarish like the elm?

To catch the 'feeling' of a tree is very difficult. You have to be sure what qualities make that tree unique. You must work this out clearly in your mind before you can have any hope of presenting it in terms of line.

If you feel that there are too many factors to be borne in mind all at once, set yourself the task of learning how to draw trees by selecting one characteristic – say, perhaps, texture – and concentrate all your thought and ability on

expressing this one aspect of the tree to the exclusion of everything else. When you fail – and you are bound to fail for a very long time – look at the tree drawings of Rembrandt and Corot to see how you may set about solving your problems.

If you can tackle the business of learning to draw in this way, by sorting out in your mind exactly what is required of the drawing instead of simply sitting down and scratching furiously at your sheet of paper, you will assimilate a technique which will be invaluable to you in every field of art. You will not be learning 'how to draw trees', you will be learning how to draw.

Suppose that instead of studying drawing by way of some natural object you should decide to draw from your imagination. This is, in a way, a more difficult way of learning to draw because the problems involved are not so clearly defined.

One such procedure is to draw something 'imaginatively' rather like a child does. You will very quickly see how limited your inventive faculty is. You will tend to fall into a certain pattern of drawing from which it is very difficult

90

91

92

to escape. Take the face as an example: it is as if one only knows of one way of drawing a nose or an eye or a mouth from memory. As soon as you become aware of this limitation you will have a 'problem' around which you can start to work. You will gradually free your inventive faculty and improve your drawing ability if you try to do a very simple drawing in an unaccustomed way.

Start out as simply as possible. Begin by drawing three faces at the top of a sheet of paper: it does not matter at this point whether the faces resemble each other or not. Now cover them up with a sheet of card so that you cannot see them, and draw three more faces at the top of another sheet of paper. Cover this paper up too and leave them for an hour or so without looking at them. After this time has elapsed, draw three more faces on a third piece of paper and then examine all the nine faces. You will find that these faces have a lot of common characteristics (plates 90-92) – it may be the shape of the face as a whole; it may be the way you draw the eyes or the mouth, it may be the proportions between all these things. You will most probably have drawn all the faces in the same type of line.

These nine faces give you some material upon which you can work. Take several small sheets of drawing paper and on each one draw your face *each time making one alteration*. On the first sheet you may draw ten or fifteen faces each with a different type of nose. You will have noted already how you tend to draw only one kind of nose, so you must be on your guard against this and try to invent as many different ones as you can for the same face. When you have filled about six sheets with as many different alterations as possible, select the type of face you like most of all and do a series of variations on this one. If you find that it is quite impossible to invent new ways of drawing noses or some other part of the face, take a look at the drawings of Paul Klee (plate 94) or at some primitive masks (plate 3), for in these the inventive faculty is superbly evident, and you can often adapt such ideas for your own work.

Once you have come to terms with this kind of inventive drawing, and you have caught a glimpse of the mechanical way in which we draw if we do not continually exercise our imagination, you can go on to other subjects than faces. Try, for example, to draw a series of whimsical animals or

93 Rembrandt, 'Portrait of the Artist's Mother', etching. By courtesy of The Trustees of The British Museum, London

94 Klee, 'Child Consecrated to Suffering'. Room of Contemporary Art, Albright-Knox Art Gallery, Buffalo, New York © S.P.A.D.E.M. Paris, 1965

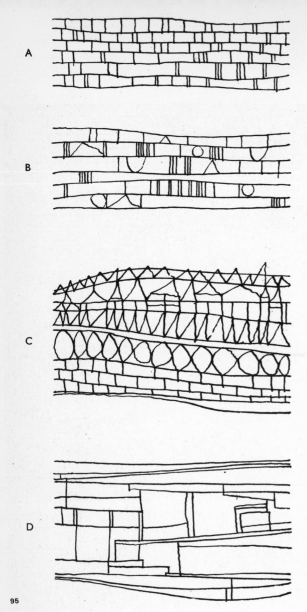

A

B

C

D

95

96

97

fishes. Klee appears to have been particularly fond of drawing exotic fish. A useful exercise would be for you to copy one of his fish drawings, like those in his painting *Fish Magic* on plate 96, and then to do a series of imaginative developments on it, until you arrive at a fish of your own. The series of drawings on plate 98 will give you some idea of how you can develop an initial idea.

Regal Fish (plate 99) is an example of how exotic a form may become after a whole series of imaginative steps.

The use of abstract line brings quite a different range of problems to be solved. Again we shall have to start simply if we wish to learn anything. The simplest line is, of course, the straight line without any significant texture, so let us begin by drawing a series of roughly parallel lines. Now fill in each of these areas between the lines with very simple patterns – even squares and oblongs (Figure A, plate 95). Figures A, B and C show basic variations on this method. The horizontal lines may also be varied (Diagram D, plate 95) so that they have different lengths, and the vertical lines may be drawn so as to create a system of interlocking shapes. With this method of drawing

it is possible to make fantastic animals, human beings and buildings, like Klee's drawing on plate 97.

Another interesting way of producing a good line drawing is really nothing more than extended 'doodling'. Take a sheet of good drawing card and trace on it a rectangle in faint pencil line about four inches by six. Now stick four pieces of sellotape along the outer perimeter of the rectangle to prevent any of the ink lines you are going to draw from crossing the pencil line. Now start to draw with a very fine pen: draw any simple shape you like – a circle or a star, and then fill the shape in with a detailed pattern. Do this, using different shapes and patterns, at other points in the rectangle, and when you have about twenty of these start to fill in the remaining blank paper with little patterns. You should finish up with a drawing something like the one on plate 100. A similar method of drawing is to start at the top left hand corner of your rectangle and to work right across the top with doodle patterns until you reach the right hand corner, at which point you retrace your steps and begin to draw from left to right once more, as if the pencil were reading a book.

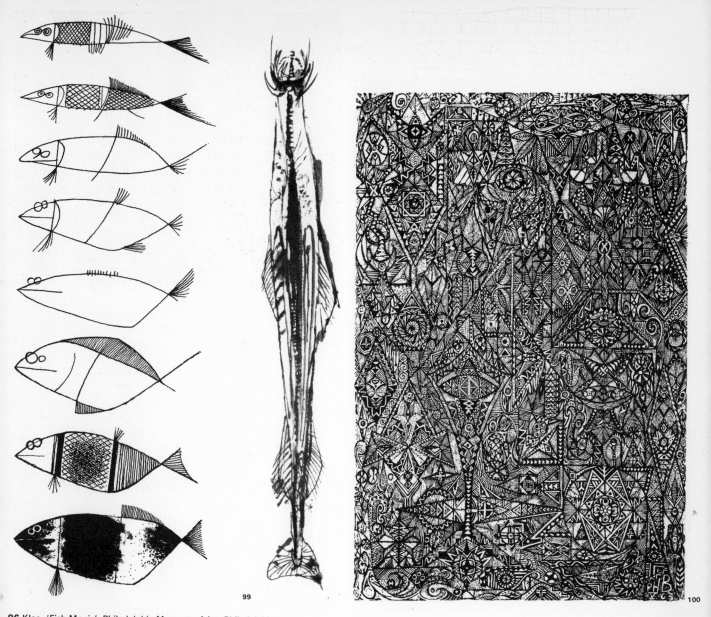

99

100

96 Klee, 'Fish Magic'. Philadelphia Museum of Art, Philadelphia
  ⓒ S.P.A.D.E.M. Paris, 1965

97 Klee, 'The Great Dome'. The Paul Klee Foundation, Kunstmuseum, Berne
  ⓒ S.P.A.D.E.M. Paris, 1965

99 Fred Gettings. 'Regal Fish'. Author's collection

100 Robert Browne, 'Doodle Drawing'. Private collection

Colour

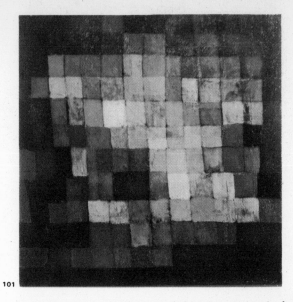

101 Klee, 'Ancient Sound'. Doetsch Benziger Bequest, Kupferstichkabinett, Kunstmuseum, Basel © S.P.A.D.E.M. Paris, 1965   101

Colour is something of a problem. It is the most changeable of all things because it is the measure of light. Colour is a problem for the landscape artist desperately combating its transiency; it is a problem for the abstract artist because it cannot be categorised or even understood, and it is a problem for the art theorist because it is an experience and not a thing.

One of the paradoxical ways of presenting the scientific theory of colour is to say that the colour an object is said to possess is the very colour it does not have. Colour is the sensation, the brain interpretation, of those light waves which impinge on the rods and cones of our retina. These light waves are the ones rejected by external objects. Such considerations may be regarded as being out of place in a chapter on colour in art, but in fact they are of pre-eminent importance, for the interaction between object and cerebral interpretation is the basis of aesthetic experience.

Outdoor changes of light, the nature of our perceptions and the movement of our planet, condition our lives. The intensity and colour created by a less fluctuating artificial light alter with the rhythm of our breathing and with our movement. The colour of a wall is not the same at a distance of two feet as it is at four or eight. Light, and thus colour, is essentially transient.

If the colour of a wall with an undifferentiated surface can change with our distance and sensitivity, how much more so can a picture with an intricate colour scheme. The light intensity (varying, so we are told, inversely with the square root of distance) is the least of our problems: it is the air, that thin refracting film of dust particles, which comes between our eyes and the object which conditions the light and colour with its game of flux which is our main problem. In one effect of light, and at a certain distance, a picture may be beautiful. A slight change, perhaps the passing of a cloud, and the colour is less pleasant. Certain private galleries, anxious to sell their wares, understand such tricks of lighting: with a judicious placing of lamps and careful background arrangement a picture of more than questionable merit may appear quite beautiful.

One may question this flux which is at the root of our world of experience, but ignore its implications. One may observe a work of art drained of its colour as a beam of sunlight moves across it, and the assumption is that there is a picture of a certain colour arrangement which is being temporarily spoiled. The truth is that since the picture experience can only exist in terms of light, it is changing all the time. The 'picture' is a series of experiences of varying degrees of intensity.

A real understanding of the implications of this 'flux' will enable a student to develop an open attitude of mind to every work of art, so that its uniqueness as an object in time and space may filter through, and with it, perhaps, a direct aesthetic experience.

Pure colour is as much an impossibility as a static work of art. Light rays which spring from what may in origin be a pure hue are played havoc with by a multitude of molecular forces the moment it sets out on its journey to the eye. Once it has reached the eye and is translated to the brain further adulteration takes place. Our associative system intervenes and labels the colour with a name and connotation, and then our emotional system makes a judgement as to whether it is pleasant or unpleasant, warm or cold, in harmony with its surroundings, and so on.

Around this optical and emotionally reactive system of ours various 'colour theories' have been constructed which attempt to classify colours into groups and systems. Colour presents so many real difficulties both in theory and in practice that it will be rewarding for us to examine the more elementary aspects of such theories before attempting to come to grips with colour in actual practice.

Colour is referred to in terms of both tone and hue. *Tone* is the light and dark value of the colour as opposed to the hue: it can best be understood by imagining a series of gradations from black to white – these two, and the intermediary greys, are tones. Colours may be gradated tonally in a similar way: a colour may be said to be dark or light in tone. *Tonal values* are the compared relationship between different tones. *Hue* is, in its strictest sense, a colour obtained by mixing a primary colour with a secondary one (see below), but in a more general sense it refers to the colour as opposed to the tone. A hue may be strong or weak: a bright red, for example, is of a strong hue.

The Primary colours are YELLOW, RED and BLUE. These

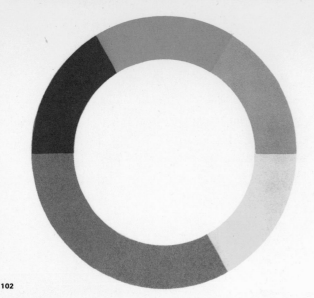

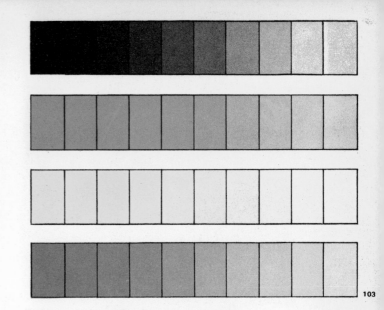

102
103

are the three colours from which all others are formed. When any two primary colours are mixed together in any proportions, Secondary colours are obtained. When, for example, YELLOW and RED are mixed, an ORANGE is produced, ORANGE being a secondary colour. The hue of this ORANGE will depend on the proportions of YELLOW and RED in its composition.

The range of hues which may be obtained by intermixing the three primaries are, of course, without limit, but, as can be seen from plate 104, for the sake of simplicity, we can think of these as consisting of six different hues. These have been arranged into a definite sequence of intermixings: RED merges into a pure hue of YELLOW. YELLOW merges into GREEN, GREEN merges into BLUE and BLUE merges back into RED. Each of these successive stages of mixing is sometimes then subjected to tonal gradations by the systematic addition of white which has the effect of weakening the hue and lightening the tone of each colour.

Complementary colours are those directly opposite each other on the circle. RED is, for example, the complement of GREEN, and the two colours are contrasts. When any two complementary colours are mixed together they produce a *Neutral* which varies in colour between grey and brown depending on the proportions of the two complements. A mixture of complements in a fifty-fifty proportion will produce a black.

Among the commonplace 'optical illusion' tricks there is one which demonstrates the complementary action of colour. If we stare at a strong hue of ORANGE for about fifteen seconds and then turn our eyes to a blank white surface a BLUE spot will appear on that surface. Complements are contrasts, and when two complementary colours are placed next to each other they 'clash' and appear to be vibrating.

Colours are said to be 'warm' and 'cool'. The 'warmest' colours are in the top half of the circle, and the coldest in the bottom half. Cool colours are below the horizontal diameter, warm ones above. There is no explanation as to why colours should have degrees of 'warmth', but the most common suggestion is that we associate ORANGE-YELLOW with the warmth of a flame and that BLUE is the colour of

104

shadows on snow, but this is by no means a very satisfactory suggestion, for very hot metal is a 'white' and so is cold snow and ice.

It is strongly recommended that the student should experiment with colour mixing at this stage. Nothing very complicated is demanded, but he should become familiar with the proportions of primary colours which are required to obtain specific secondary hues. A good experiment would be to start out only with the three primaries, and paint a series of juxtaposed squares in different tones and warmths from the intermixing of complementaries. If you take a piece of card or good quality paper and draw on it a series of seventy squares, seven by ten in proportion, your task should be to fill each of the squares with a colour as near as possible in hue and tone, yet all obtained by different intermixings. This is only possible in theory, but one should, after a little effort, be able to approximate to the ideal. If you find this experiment too difficult to complete with any success, you could limit yourself to trying to mix three areas of colour side by side of exactly the same hue and tone, and again all obtained by different intermixings. Such exercises

as these will develop not only your mixing ability, but also heighten your colour awareness.

Another way to learn about colour is to experiment in the following way. Draw a series of squares and rectangles something along the lines of those shown in A, B or D in plate 95. Trace this drawing and make a number of copies onto separate sheets of cartridge paper. When you have seven or eight copies of the same drawing you can begin to fill in the squares with colour.

On the first drawing you should limit yourself to one colour only. Try to fill in each of the squares with a different tone by mixing the paint afresh for each square. Take the second drawing and limit yourself to two colours – preferably two harmonising colours like green and brown – and by intermixing or using them separately try to paint a pleasant arrangement of colours. The aim of both these experiments is to paint a picture with as much tonal variety as possible.

By doing these two simple experiments you should have found out several things. The most obvious thing you will have seen is how relatively easy it is to paint a pleasant picture in one colour. Beginners usually rush madly at their

108

paint boxes and try to put into their pictures a little bit of
every colour. If you examine the paintings of the great
masters like Rembrandt and Titian you will begin to
appreciate the subtle possibilities involved in a restricted
colour palette. You should also have learned that for the two
paintings to become 'pictures' as opposed to being merely
squares of colour they would need some focal point, some
centre of interest which will retain the eye. This can best be
appreciated by painting your third drawing, again limiting
yourself to one colour, in a very definite way. Start by filling
in the square nearest the centre in your palest tint of blue
(Prussian Blue is the best in this instance because it has a
wide tonal range). Now paint in the squares around this
square with a slightly darker tone (each one slightly
different in tone). These squares are to be the focal point of
your picture. You should now carry on filling in all the
other squares with considerably darker tones until the
picture is complete. If you now compare this one with the
first painting you did you will quickly grasp the importance
of a focal point.

Now try one or two experiments to get the 'feel' of

105 'Bad and Good Colours' by Melissa Ulfane, aged 7. Author's collection

106 'The War' by David Penny, aged 7, St. Johns Roman Catholic School,
Tiverton Devon. Reproduced by courtesy of the Sunday Mirror

108 'Magic Squares' by Duncan Baxter, aged 6. Author's collection

109

109 Klee, 'Garden in Bloom'. Werner Allenbach collection, Berne
ⓒ S.P.A.D.E.M. Paris, 1965

110 Richard P. Lohse, '30 systematically arranged rows of colour tones
1955/63'. Collection of the Artist

It is interesting to compare this exciting picture with the Klee on the opposite page. Although Lohse certainly owes much to his compatriot in style, his approach is in fact visibly different; whereas Klee arrived at his pictorial solution intuitively with the emphasis on feeling and an emotional groping for expression, Lohse sets out to create pictures in a more intellectual manner with the emphasis on a more systematic mental search for a solution to his well considered problem; the pronounced surface tension, the interweaving movement in and out of the picture, is calculated and not related to any specific pictorial aim, and is the direct outcome of the systematic experimentation which characterises the work of this artist.

colours. We all know that red is an exciting colour to look at. The young boy who painted 'War' instinctively understood the significance of colour, for it is purely the emotive quality of the red which makes this picture 'work' in communicating the child's excitement about his imagined air combat. Try painting one of your drawings to make it as exciting as possible with bright reds, oranges and all the other warm colours. You should be able to make a good focal point out of a pure hue of yellow. Once this is finished try painting a 'cool' picture of blues and slate greys. This has to be a soothing picture, so gradate the tonal changes gently, and avoid great clashes of contrast between the hues and tones.

Plate 105 is the result of a child's attempt to express the feeling of colour. She was asked to fill one square with 'bad' colours and another square with 'good' colours. You might try to think up a title for a picture and try to express the title in terms of coloured squares: think of the different possible combinations which could be used to evoke the atmosphere of 'Sea Storm', 'Zoo', 'Funfair' or 'Autumn'. Paul Klee painted a whole series of pictures made from

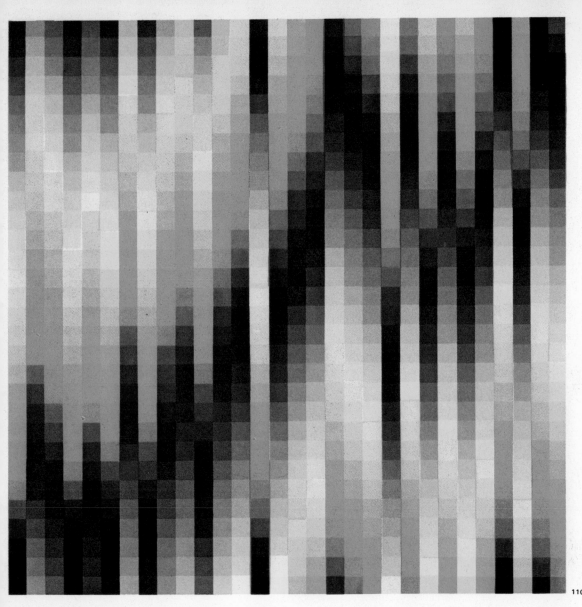

110

coloured squares which he called 'Magic Squares'. His *Garden in Bloom* is absolutely masterly in its use of colour. The centre of interest is a lovely contrast of reds, blues and yellows, all of which suggest the colourful world of flowers, whilst the surrounding background of larger areas of less gay green, browns and purples suggest the quiet generating force of the world of creation which is nature. The focal point of bright colours has a very curious 'movement' about it: Klee placed red squares next to blue ones because he knew that the red would advance and the blue recede, thus creating a depth of tensions so that the picture area would appear to be vibrating with life. The contrast between these colours and between the different sizes of the squares result in a surface tension over the picture which is very easily felt. The patch of bright colours appear to be forcing themselves out of the picture rather like flowers forcing themselves out of the earth.

When you have filled all your squares with different colour themes you can try out another series of exercises. Take a plain sheet of paper and brush onto it a dab of bright red and a few inches away a dab of bright green. These two colours

create a disharmony between them, and it is your problem to so paint the rest of the paper that the 'clash' between these colours disappears and a harmony is established. 'Give me mud', said one great painter, 'and provided I may surround it as I wish I will make of it the skin of Venus.' A colour has significance and emotional strength only in relation to its background. This can easily be verified by painting six squares of the same colour – say green – onto one sheet of paper and then painting a thick outline of different colours around five of the green squares. You will be astonished to see how different each of the green squares look against their different backgrounds.

Now paint a large square of dull colour, like buff, and allow it to dry. On top of this buff paint lots of little squares in different colours so that they look something like the colours in plate 101. You will find that the neutral background helps the colours to cohere much more satisfactorily than pure white paper does. This is because each colour is surrounded by a common element (the buff background) which gives it a certain unity. Painting in thick slabs of gouache onto black card always looks very

effective, particularly so, if you can establish a harmonious relationship between all the colours.

In an earlier exercise we set ourselves the problem of surrounding two squares of red and green so as to remove the disharmony between them. A fairly easy solution to this problem would have been to paint several different coloured squares all over the paper and surrounding the green and red, leaving about a quarter of an inch gap between them. The white channels surrounding all the colours should then be painted in black so that a network of thick black lines runs all over the picture area, uniting all the coloured squares together. This sort of design is called *cloisonné* and is reminiscent of stained glass painting where the black lines of the structural elements used to support the glass are combined with non-structural black lines which, by contrast with the translucent colours of the glass, heighten the overall colour effect. The black lines on your painting will have a similar effect: they will intensify the colour and at the same time help to bind the design together.

If you take one of the drawings which you did earlier,

whilst experimenting with line, and colour it with bright hues and textured colours, and then retrace the original pen lines with black lines of various thicknesses you will see something of the value of black paint. It is the black division lines on the enchanting picture of a steam boat on plate 111 which make the colour so translucent and so unified, but the force of this effect is so strong that one scarcely notices the black at all.

111 'Steam Boat', Group work by children aged 12-14, Firrhill Secondary School, Edinburgh, Scotland. Reproduced by courtesy of the Sunday Mirror

Composition

113

The word 'composition' is derived from the Latin *componere*, which means 'to put together', and when we talk about the composition of a picture we refer to the manner in which all the different elements of colour, form, texture and design have been combined into a whole. Thus a composition may be as complex as an immense canvas by Rubens or as simple as a rectilinear painting made from a few lines and colours by Mondrian.

A good composition is one in which all the different elements of the particular art form have been integrated to achieve a very definite effect. The composition should reveal, either directly or indirectly, the *intention* of the artist, and if it fails to do this it may be considered to be a bad composition. Obviously one must exercise great care in the evaluation of a work of art, for unless one understands the aim of the artist in creating a particular work, one is not in a good position to make judgments about it. For this reason it is essential that the function of composition, which is so intimately connected with the artist's intention, be correctly understood. This is necessary not only for the commonsense approach to art in practice, but also for the proper understanding of art theory and history.

Compositional forms may thus be defined in terms of artistic intention. This leads to the possibility of superficially similar paintings belonging to entirely different categories, but in general terms there is a clear distinction between the forms which emerge if we analyse them closely. There are three basic compositional forms which have been called Decorative, Representational and Expository. They are only rarely found in isolation and are usually combined in different degrees within the same work of art. We shall examine each of these forms in some detail, attempt to understand the principles involved and then try to produce one or two works in terms of these three categories.

The most common compositional form is called the Decorative. This does not merely refer to repetitive pattern, to which the word 'decoration' is sometimes applied, but to that type of composition which aims to please the spectator by direct aesthetic experience. In a decorative composition the details and components of the work are so arranged as to form a whole which pleases by its decorative impact, its colour and its formal relation. The paintings of Matisse,

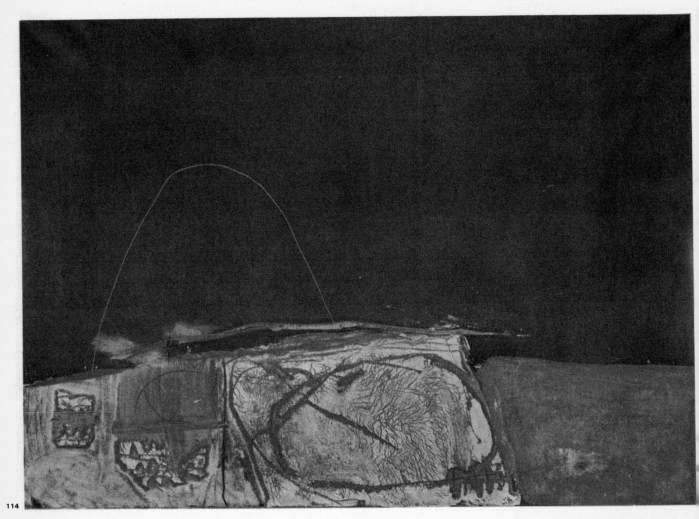

114

which exhibit a strong decorative sensibility based on shapes, repetition of motifs, and organised texture, are an excellent example of this kind of composition. Matisse summed up the aim and intention of decorative composition in an admirable way when he said that he dreamed of an art of purity and calmness, devoid of any disturbance in content, an art form 'for the business man, something like a comfortable arm chair in which one can rest from physical fatigue.' It must be understood that Matisse intends pleasure for the spectator; he does not imply necessarily that the artist should experience pleasure in the execution of the painting. Decorative composition is concerned with the pleasure involved in visual enjoyment: the stimulation of the eye in visual terms, so that the painting, both as a formal whole and as a series of passages in paint, is rather like an enjoyable piece of music.

A decorative composition may be realistic, semi-realistic or completely abstract, but in each case its aim will be the same: to provoke pleasure. The group painting of the steamboat is as representative of this compositional form as the abstract painting by the Spanish artist Tapies (plate 114).

The second compositional form is called Representational, and takes as its aim the description of the familiar world of experience. An artist who paints in a representational style delights in pointing out such aspects of nature which arouse a sense of beauty, wonder and enthusiasm. Clearly, portraiture is one class of art which falls within this category, for the aim of a portrait painter is to describe the external character of the sitter. The painting of Cézanne, so obviously an outward sign of an attempt to 'realise sensations', is one of the highest expressions of this compositional form, for all the details of colour, form and design combine to describe the reality perceived by the artist.

Representational composition may be realistic, semirealistic, and even abstract, provided its aim is to describe an aspect of the visible appearance of things. While it is not necessary to argue a case for Rembrandt, for example, who was one of the finest of representational painters, a more subtle approach is required to understand why a painting like the one by da Silva (plate 115) may be described as belonging to this category. What at first sight may appear to be a picture in the decorative tradition, an abstract

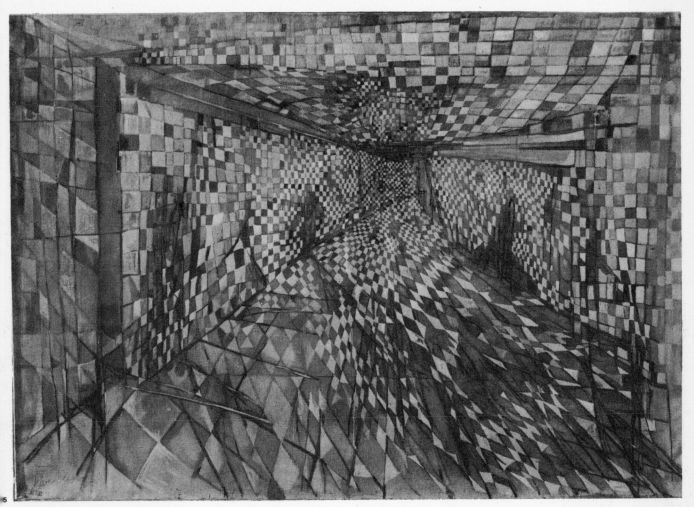

arrangement of harlequin shapes in grey and silver, is in fact concerned with describing an aspect of reality. We do not see this at first because the method da Silva employs is not a familiar one. The subject is a corridor, but da Silva does not concern herself merely with describing the dimensions, colour, texture and depth of the corridor in the usual way: she attempts to describe *what happens* in this corridor. One can feel the continual movement of people along the passage way, some hurrying, some merely walking. One gets an impression of doors opening and closing along the corridor walls, with people continually flitting in and out. All this is a description in unfamiliar terms of what happens within the familiar world of experience.

   The third type of compositional form is called Expository, and takes as its aim the explanation of general relationships, abstract meanings and causal connections. Religious painting, which is concerned with the exposition of doctrines and beliefs, is in this class. Michelangelo's Sistine Chapel, Signorelli's *Last Judgment* in Orvieto Cathedral, and, to stay within the Renaissance, Botticelli's *Primavera*, are all superb examples of this type of composition, for

they are each highly organised mystical allegories. As we shall see later, such artists as Turner (plate 116) occasionally painted in expository terms. Several modern art forms are concerned with expository composition: the Surrealists, for example, attempt to reveal the meaning of the subconscious manifestations of the human mind in the creative act, so that, as a more precise example, a picture by Max Ernst may be concerned with explaining in pictorial terms the post-Freudian theories connected with the periodic influence of the lunar cycle on the human psyche.

   Expository composition is always didactic and is closely connected with symbolism. It, too, may be realistic, semi-realistic and even abstract. Whilst it is easy to see how Raphael's *Crucifixion* may fall into this category, it is not so easy for us to understand how the painting in plate 117 may be placed in this class. A brief examination might suggest that it should be classified as a decorative composition, consisting as it does of flat areas of colour arranged in a pleasant design, and obviously intended to decorate a particular room (plate 16). If, however, we relate this picture to the aims I had in mind when I painted it, we

116

should be able to see why it is an expository composition.

The painting is an attempt to present a philosophical idea in terms of simple pictorial symbolism. When I set out to paint it I was very much concerned with the study of pictorial tension, and being impressed by Paracelsus's statement that 'Man is the mid-point between Heaven and Earth', I decided to attempt a pictorial equivalent of this idea, employing certain tensional devices. The green shape at the bottom represents the Earth – green as a symbol of vegetative growth, and the breast-like form on the left of the shape is suggestive of maternity, Mother Earth, and the female principle in life. The whole shape emerges from the base of the picture, suggesting the emergence of Earth from the lower spheres of the Universe. Thus, as a whole, the shape symbolises the female principle of Earth as a reservoir of vegetative life. The large yellow shape on the right is symbolic of the Sun as life-giver and maintainer of planetary movement. Yellow is the colour most obviously associated with the Sun and stars, with what Paracelsus called 'The upper sphere' as opposed to the 'lower sphere' of Earth. The shape is symbolic of Heaven. In form it is phallic, and is therefore to be identified with the male principle of creation, while the way it runs off the picture is suggestive of the fact that we see only a fragment of a much larger thing. At the point where the green and yellow shapes are nearest, and where there is a surface tension between the forces, I placed a white shape, which is, symbolically, generated by the male and female force of Earth and Heaven. This shape is a symbol of man, the creation of the interacting forces of Heaven and Earth. Man is a duality with a body composed of Earth, and a spirit composed of the Sun. This is the meaning held in this composition which is, quite clearly, of the expository type.

Once you have begun to see the issues involved in these three compositional forms, you may be prepared to set yourself the task of painting one or two pictures in terms of the three categories.

In order to exploit the possibilities of decorative composition you might choose to do a completely abstract oil painting along the lines of the one at plate 118. If you do this you must make an effort to keep your aim in mind, which is to paint a surface with a texture and colour arrangement which is pleasant to the eye. If you try to finish the picture in one go, without waiting for the successive layers of oil paint to form a surface skin, your picture will more easily catch that spontaneous, painterly look of *Yellow Abstract*.

If you are not quite certain how to set about making an abstract picture (even after reading the chapter on Basic Design) you can follow as closely as possible the procedure described below, and make a picture of your own. Remember what you learned in your colour experiments and restrict your palette both in hue and tonal contrast. Paint broadly and directly and try to avoid any fiddling around with the brush or knife, as this will lead to a 'fussy' picture. A palette knife is probably more suitable for this kind of painting than a brush, and it may be a good idea to limit yourself in time – half an hour is quite enough – so that you do not completely lose yourself in the painting and forget why you set out to paint it.

Yellow Abstract was painted onto a prepared sheet of thick plywood which had been strengthened against warping by four wooden strips on the back. As my intention was to paint the picture in one go and to restrict my palette to one dominant colour, I laid out only four colours on to my glass 'palette'; burnt umber, yellow ochre, lemon yellow and white. First of all I spread a liberal coat of white paint unevenly on to the board with my palette knife, and then I mixed a little lemon yellow and white together and dragged it with the palette knife over the white base. This left a rather interesting streaky surface. The cold blue of the prepared board was left to show through in places because it formed a gentle contrast with the predominant yellow. Next I mixed the two yellows unevenly together, and placed a large amount on my knife and then smoothed down thick slabs of the mixture onto the centre of the board with quick knife strokes. At this point I observed that my hand had the tendency to move with a circular motion of the wrist, and so I decided to add one or two bold circular strokes to the painting in burnt umber with the tip of the palette knife. The design of the painting was by now built out of circular movements of the hand, so in order to introduce a little contrast, and also to 'marry' the design to the straight edges of the frame, I added the two straight lines which emerge

117

from the bottom of the picture rather like plant stalks. Then I cleaned the palette knife and made one or two scratches in the paint surface, splattered a little of the burnt umber from a large hog-hair brush, and the picture was complete.

You could paint an abstract picture in a similar fashion by taking some central motif (those found on carpets are usually excellent for this sort of thing) and construct a picture from this.

A different approach is for one to take a surface – either natural or man-made – and make a painterly interpretation of it as an experiment in decorative abstract work.

Plate 19 is a photograph of a wall surface left as a result of structural alterations made to one of the walls in Hampton Court. The accidental textures, the subtle colouring and the fascinating formal relationship between the jutting beam ends, caught my attention, and I decided to make a painting of it.

The first thing I had to do was to make a detailed sketch of the wall, taking great care to establish the exact distances between all the beam ends so as to preserve the exciting formal relationship between them. This I first attempted to record as a 'frottage' (see page 75) but it proved impractical because of the position of the wall texture. A more exact record than a mere free-hand sketch was required to establish the precise relationship of squares on the wall texture, so as a last resort I turned to photography and had a large copy made to help with the painting. Once all the preparatory sketches were made I listed a series of colour notes on the textures and colours of the wall surface.

By now everything was ready for work in the studio. I transferred the sketch to a hardboard sheet and then made a careful copy of the wall texture from my notes and sketches. First of all I painted the concrete surface in paint resembling both the colour and texture of the concrete without actually ruining the feel of the paint. This I did by dragging a full thick brush over the canvas grain of the hardboard, and left the mechanical texture of the board to show through only in isolated spots. Then I painted in the thick slabs of the wooden beam ends and left the whole picture in this state for a few weeks until it was reasonably dry. After that time I worked slowly on the whole canvas, staining, scratching, adding *impasto*, scumbling, adding washes of linseed or

118

119

coloured turpentine, in an effort to find a painterly equivalent for the textures and colours found on the original wall surfaces.

Instead of tackling an abstract painting you may be more inclined to attempt a realistic picture for your decorative composition. Before you begin it might be a good idea to have a close look at the work of those artists who have produced fine pictures in the 'decorative' tradition. The work of the Intimist painters Vuillard and Bonnard are by far the best examples of compositions in which all other considerations are sacrificed to a decorative formal arrangement of colours, shapes and texture.

Building Site No. 4 (plate 119) was painted (or perhaps a better word would be 'constructed') by a group of children. The strong sense of pattern and design, the lack of regard for linear or aerial perspective, and the clever use of texture, mark this as a fine example of decorative composition. The children who made the picture intended merely to please the spectator by a pleasant display of colour and form: they were not concerned with describing the familiar world, nor with 'explaining' anything in didactic terms. It is interesting

to see how they have used textured elements as an integral part of their design – string and cloth for the wheels, real sand and aggregate for the pile of sand to the left, and in the wheelbarrow and on the sandstone wall, pieces of cloth, newspaper and wood for the concrete mixer and cotton wool for the smoke puffed out by the traction engine in the foreground.

Perhaps your second attempt at decorative composition can be made something along these lines. You might, for example, choose an interior scene by Bonnard in a colour reproduction, examine it closely and then try to make a free interpretation of it in terms of some medium other than paint. Another possibility would be for you to paint a picture of the room you are working in by simplifying large areas and shapes of the things you see before you into washes of colour.

Your approach to representative composition will be largely determined by what interests you in painting. Whereas in the last exercise you attempted to paint a room in terms of decorative elements your aim might now be to *describe* that same room or something in it.

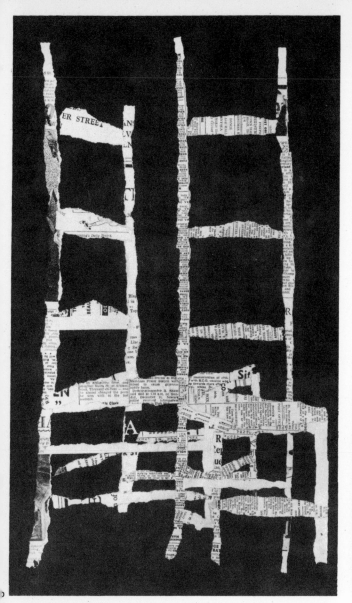

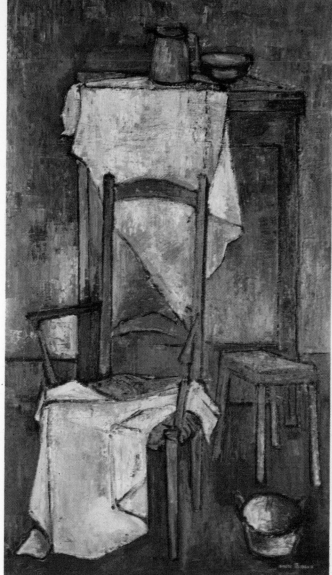

121

The collage picture of a chair on plate 120 is quite obviously decorative. The child who made the picture was interested chiefly in the flat pattern of the chair and not in describing its form and nature. If you compare this with the painting by Minaux on plate 121 you will see the basic difference in approach which marks the latter out as a representative composition. Certainly Minaux is as interested in the pattern of the chair as the child who constructed the collage, but Minaux's interest does not end there for he attempts to describe the chair as an individual object in relation to other objects. He represents the room in depth and describes the rhythm of the receding horizontal planes formed by the seat of the chair, the stool and the top of the dresser. In pointing out this relationship he is commenting on reality and describing something within the visible appearance of things. Minaux is to a certain extent following the footsteps of Van Gogh, who, it will be remembered, once painted a 'portrait' of a yellow chair: and we have already seen that portraiture falls within the class of representative composition.

You may decide to take as a subject for your representative

composition a household chair and tackle it in a similar way to Minaux. You might set yourself the problem of describing one or two of the qualities in the chair: perhaps, like Minaux, you are interested in the spatial rhythm of the chair and its surroundings, or perhaps, like Van Gogh, you are interested in its 'unique personality'. You may decide to be a little more conservative than either of these two painters and restrict yourself to describing the shape, colour, texture and form of the chair. Whichever aspect of the chair's reality you single out for attention you must be quite clear in your mind what you want to do. If you sit down and draw or paint a chair with no particular aim in mind you will achieve nothing – except a drawing or painting of a chair.

When you turn your attention to producing an expository composition you will be faced with an entirely different series of problems. By far the easiest thing to do will be to restrict your first attempt to abstract work: to invent symbols for a particular idea or series of ideas in your mind.

A symbol is the result of an attempt to preserve and convey an idea. A good pictorial symbol carries a more or less rich connotation which is, by virtue of its intrinsic nature, made clear to those who attempt to understand it. This means, of course, that pictorial symbolism is a 'language' which may be deciphered and that it is a language which must be learned.

Those people who do not trouble to learn something of the language of symbolism are not in a good position to understand symbolic art forms. Chinese art, as indeed most Far Eastern art, is composed of a highly complex and very rich symbolism, and to those in the West who are not familiar with the meaning of these symbols, Far Eastern art passes merely for so much decoration. In fact most Chinese, Japanese and Indian works of art are so unintelligible to us that they resemble writing in an unknown language. Anyone who approaches such art forms solely from the point of view of their decorative qualities and general aesthetic considerations is doing the equivalent of admiring the calligraphy on a Chinese scroll and not understanding the message contained within the scroll.

The problem of communication – of how to understand the symbols used by the artist – is the fundamental problem of art appreciation. There is always a gap between what the artist has to say and how he says it, but there is a chasm between what he says and how he is interpreted. The work of art is a sort of interpreter between the artist and his audience, and for this reason the study of symbolism, both in theory and in practical exercises, is of paramount importance to artistic development.

The strength and meaning of a symbol is directly related to the intention of the artist. The texture picture at plate 123 for example would be so much nonsense to someone not aware of the artist's intention. Again, suppose a naturalist drew a picture of a snake coiled around a tree trunk, we could assume that he was working in the representative tradition with the intention of making a descriptive 'catalogue' of the appearance of the snake. However, should another person draw a snake coiled around a tree trunk, with an apple near by and intend the snake to refer to the temptation of Eve in the Garden of Eden, then the snake would belong to an entirely different order of art. Whilst this second snake may be just as descriptively accurate as the first the intention of the artist has entirely changed its significance. To condemn the second drawing on the grounds of, say, anatomical inaccuracy would be to miss the whole point of the drawing. Such an example enables one to see very clearly the importance of trying to grasp the intention of the artist before assessing the value of his work.

At exactly what point a descriptive painting turns into a symbolical painting is extremely difficult to determine. Turner painted many pictures which might be taken as descriptive passages in a rather abstract style, but which on further analysis turn out to be immense symbols of Nature's force (plate 116). His contemporary, Blake, evolved a whole system of closely-knit symbols of a verbal and pictorial nature, because he felt that the earlier symbols then in current use for Christian ideology, such as the cross and religious personages (plate 122), had outgrown their original intensity and were out of date. Both Turner and Blake were intending to convey a meaning over and above the mere appearance of what they painted and both produced pictures of an expository nature, but whereas Blake's work is quite obviously of a symbolical nature, Turner's full significance is not immediately apparent.

In your approach to expository composition you must try to be as simple as possible, for it is the most difficult of the three compositional forms to handle. By far the easiest thing to do will be to restrict your first attempt to the abstract expression of some simple idea.

The simplest form of expository art is the diagram. In a diagram of an electric circuit, for example, certain symbols stand for the battery, ammeter, resistances and wiring system, and all of these are connected and related in a symbolical form so as to convey a definite meaning to anyone who has taken the trouble to learn a little about electricity.

The arrow is a diagram of force, as Klee knew so well (see plate 124). Perhaps you could experiment within the field of abstract expository composition by making several pictures from arrows, taken as representing some directional flow of forces. You might, for example, take a concept like 'if one directional force meets another directional force a new and different directional force is established', and try to represent the idea graphically. The graphic design at plate 125 is an excellent solution to the problem of symbols in visually an intellectual concept. We can all very well understand with our heads the significance of the phrase 'effective communication' but for us to discover a telling visual equivalent to symbolise these word symbols would be extremely difficult.

122

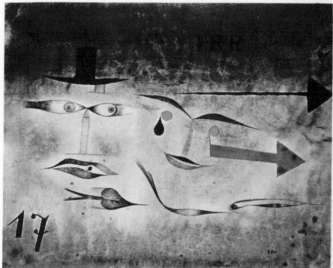

124

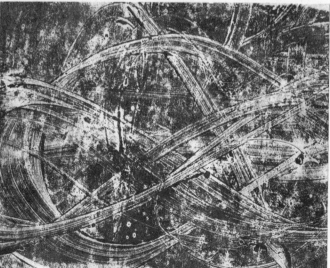

123

125

122 A page from the Book of Kells, 'The Arrest of Christ'. By permission of the Board of Trinity College, Dublin

123 Fred Gettings, 'Study in Motion'. Author's collection

124 Klee, 'Seventeen, Crazy'. Doetsch Benziger Bequest, Kupferstich-kabinett, Kunstmuseum, Basel. ©S.P.A.D.E.M. Paris, 1965

125 Brian Cowser, design for 'Effective Communication' from Liberal Studies published by Pergamon Press, in the Commonwealth Library Series

Simple Printing Methods

There is absolutely no reason why you should restrict your study of art to drawing and painting methods for there are numerous ways of making prints without having recourse to expensive materials and equipment.

The printing methods which I shall discuss here may be divided broadly into two kinds: printing directly from a roller, and printing directly from a previously rolled surface. By far the most popular of these two methods, especially with young children, is the first, because the results are achieved with so little preparation and because there is an almost magical quality in the way in which the image appears so unexpectedly on the paper. Such simple prints as thumb-prints (plate 128) may be a source of great pleasure to young children.

We shall experiment first of all with printing directly from a roller. Although a small hand roller is useful, by far the best results are obtained with a lithographic roller which is rather like a rolling pin coated with a sheet of rubber. If you are able to afford one of these rollers you must remember to make two little tubular 'gloves' out of leather which can be placed over both the handles to prevent friction with the skin of the hand. The small hand roller is not so satisfactory, but provided it is a long one (which is to say at least six inches in length) quite good results may be obtained. The main disadvantage with a hand roller is that the area it will roll in one revolution is very small. For the sake of pure experiment, however, a cheap roller will suffice. This can usually be purchased at a decorator's shop.

Before you begin your experiments roll out a good supply of printing ink on to a sheet of glass and place within easy reach a good pile of paper – flimsy typing paper is quite good for the purpose. Printing is a messy business and it is as well to wear some sort of apron to protect your clothes.

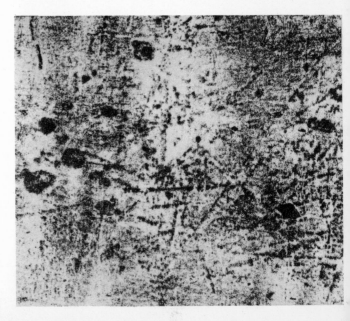

There are basically three different methods of obtaining texture with the aid of a roller. The first is by rolling with ink over a piece of paper which is itself placed over a textured surface. The second is by scratching some design or mark directly onto the roller or onto the inked slab before rolling; and the third method is by rolling over paper which has on its surface various odds and ends which prevent the ink from touching the paper, and which usually stick to the roller. It is, of course, possible to

130

131

132

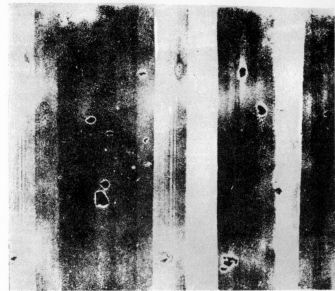

combine these three printing methods.

If you wish to obtain a texture by rolling a piece of paper on a textured surface try first of all with an accidental form, like an old drawing board, as shown in plate 126. You can then try with pieces of cloth, grained wood, a smooth surface which has been scattered with a film of sand, and indeed anything else you can find lying around. After you have experimented with accidental textures you can try manufacturing some of your own. In plate 129 the texture has been obtained by rolling over squares of paper which have been arranged on another piece of paper. Perhaps you could try a similar technique by rolling over a piece of cotton thread. It is not absolutely essential that one should use a roller in order to get good effects in this way. One can rub a pencil or crayon over raised surfaces to create good texture in much the same way as children rub carbon dust or a thick pencil onto a sheet of paper over a penny in order to make a black and white copy of the coin. Max Ernst made an enormous collection of pencil and ink rubbings of textured surfaces which he called 'frottages' – a method he described as 'conjuring up of the

shadow or ghost of an anonymous object to find therein an imaginative stimulus'. Plates 131 and 136 show how one might experiment with making frottages. The rubbing at plate 135 was obtained by rubbing black crayon directly over a piece of paper laid on a slab of grained wood. The 'rubbing' (plate 132) is a direct impression obtained by pressing down an inked fern onto the paper. The print (plate 136) is being made by rubbing a crayon over a sheet of paper placed on top of a small pavement grate.

Although the end product is quite different, the 'frottage' method is exactly the same as that used in making rubbings from monumental brasses and tombstones. The ancient Chinese had a most interesting way of making 'frottages' of a more controlled nature than that which interested Ernst. They would carve into stone some design (most often a linear copy of a painting or brush drawing) and then spread a fine dampened paper over the top of the stone. Then they would press the dampened paper lightly into the engraved lines and leave it to dry. Afterwards they rolled ink lightly over the paper surface so that the paper which had been indented into the grooves was left

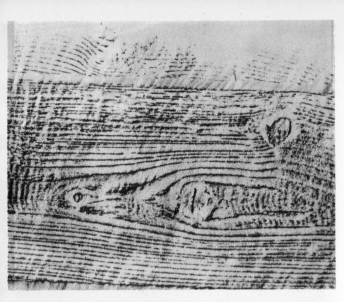

138

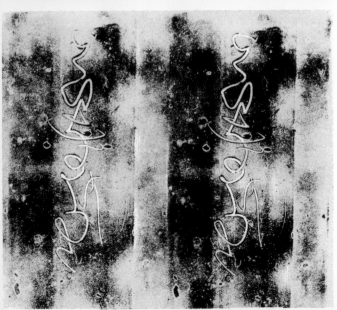

139

140

139 Print by Dawn Broome, aged 8. Author's collection

140 Fred Gettings, 'Glimpse into Order'. Collection of Peter Stanford, Leicester University

141 Print by Briony Ensor, aged 6. Author's collection

142 Fred Gettings, 'People Entering the Gates of a Tube'. Author's collection

white against a black surface.

If you scratch into the surface of the inked roller with a matchstick and then roll the ink onto a sheet of paper, you will get an effect something like the one on plate 137. This method is best when you want to obtain a lively reversed-white line, but equally good effects can be obtained by lightly scratching the surface of the inked roller with a knife-edge, or even by smearing it with paper. Rather nice effects can be achieved by allowing pieces of fluff to fall onto the rolling slab and then rolling them well into the ink. When they are rolled over the paper they print in dark blobs with a white edging round.

If you place a small sheet of glass on a white sheet of paper and then cover it with a thin coat of ink you can draw some pattern or motif onto the surface which may clearly be seen because of the white paper beneath the glass. A reversed print can be taken from this drawing by placing a sheet of paper on the glass and rubbing firmly down with your fingers. Before peeling the paper from the glass completely, examine one corner of the print to see if

it has received enough pressure to make a good contrast with the white drawing (plate 138).

An interesting technique which is hardly printing but which my young pupils find most interesting is that of placing a sheet of paper face down on a sheet of glass charged with ink and then drawing lightly over the back of this paper with a stylus. Plates 139 and 141 show something of the results which can be obtained with this method.

Textures which give an impression of movement and speed can be obtained by hitting the paper with the inked roller, sometimes dragging it along, sometimes twisting it and at other times touching the paper with only one end of the roller (plate 140).

People Entering the Gates of the Tube at plate 142 was 'painted' chiefly by this method, with a little additional splatter work and touching up with a pen. The lettering on the walls and offices was obtained by wax rubbing (see page 96). This painting was the result of a morning's observation at Oxford Circus Tube Station, where I tried to catch the movement of the crowd and work out the best way of painting the movement, bustle and excitement of the

crowd. I also wanted to suggest something of the horror of the tube station which appeared to be a miniature gateway to hell, and the people rushing into it, insubstantial ghosts. Numerous attempts to paint or draw what I felt failed miserably, and it was only after I started to use this particular kind of texture that my aim was achieved. In this way the movement of the people, all travelling at different speeds, the immobility of the gates, and even the noise, was suggested without having to resort to a technique of 'cinematographic overlapping' which is the easiest way of suggesting movement.

A blob or smear of ink may be rolled over once with a clean roller and will print in a most exciting way (plate 144). The accidental shapes obtained in this manner are often very beautiful, but their sizes are limited by the size of the roller.

Once you have learned something about the variety of textures which may be created with a roller you can start combining methods in different colours so as to make actual pictures.

Extra Mundane Figure (plate 143) was made with a

143

144

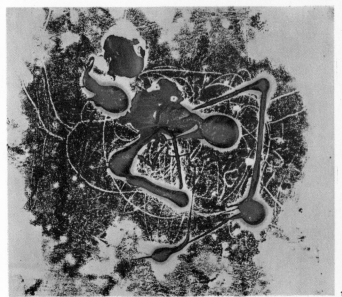

14

lithographic roller. First of all I rolled a thin stain of lithographic ink over the rolling slab, then I splashed a few drops of turpentine over the ink so as to increase its tonal range, then I touched up the slab with a few blobs of black ink from a palette knife. After I had splattered a little of the black ink onto the slab I rolled a clean roller once over the whole area taking care to ensure that I completed one revolution only. I then transferred the ink onto a clean sheet of paper by running the roller over it once. The white edges around the thick black areas were a little disconcerting so I subdued them by allowing the picture to dry for several days and then brushing a thin coat of clear varnish over the whole design. The oil in the varnish toned down the white of the paper to a subtle brown and brought out the intense richness of the red.

The three 'prints' at plates 145, 146 and 147 were all made by my young pupils in my studio.

Printing with a roller is exciting and requires the minimum of equipment and preparation but it has the serious limitation of not really being a printing method. It is difficult to make more than two or three prints from any

one design by any of the methods described above. Since the drawing is done in terms of the film of ink on the roller or on the glass the number of prints will depend on how long this film will last.

Printing from a previously rolled surface is a much more versatile method than the one we have just examined. It has the advantage of being more rewarding in that there is no serious limitation to the number of prints one can take. Whereas in the first method the number of prints from any particular design is strictly limited by the technique itself, in the second method the number of prints depends entirely on the durability of the block from which they are made. The rolled ink in this case is merely a medium for recording an impression – a transmitting agent – and not an intrinsic part of the print itself.

There are two main forms of printing from a rolled surface – one which is called *relief* printing, in which the image to be printed is raised so as to receive a thin film of ink from a roller; and another form called *intaglio* printing in which the image to be printed is eaten or bitten into the surface so as to form a complex of fine channels

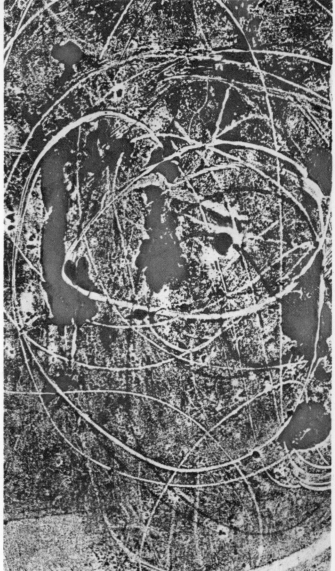

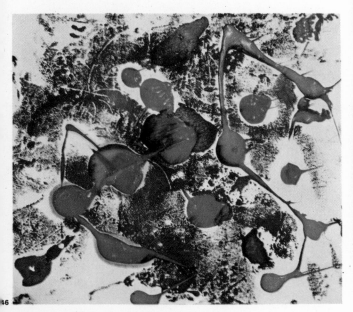

which will hold the ink which is subsequently pressed into the paper under considerable pressure. The principle of relief printing is best seen in the finger print (plate 128), which leaves a delicate record of the raised epidermal ridges of the skin: it is the most commonly used of printing methods and embraces letterpress, the woodcut, wood-engraving and lino printing. The most common forms of intaglio printing are line-engraving and etching.

For each of these methods a heavy press is an essential piece of equipment in order to obtain the correct pressures required by the different methods, but in certain cases, particularly in relief work, in which a print is made as a result of a kiss between a raised inked surface and the paper, it is possible to dispense with a press and use a dry roller or pressure with the back of a spoon. Intaglio printing is based on the principle that ink retained in fine engraved channels is forced under high pressure onto the paper (in fact it is the paper fibre which is forced into the engraved channels) and a high pressure press is therefore necessary for this type of printing. We shall examine only one method which uses an intaglio process

with an ordinary nipping press.

The most popular – though most certainly not the easiest – of relief techniques is lino printing. This method, in its simplest form, consists of cutting into the surface of a piece of linoleum in order to leave a raised area to receive a coating of ink which is then transferred to paper.

Materials required for lino printing are a few sheets of lino, several cutting tools, a roller, ink and paper. A good thick piece of linoleum can be purchased at most art dealers. It is, of course, more economical to buy a large roll of printing linoleum and to cut off pieces as required, but most shops stock several standard sizes which may be purchased for a few pence. Lino may be bought mounted or unmounted. The mount consists usually of a wooden block made from plywood or laminated board which adds a rigidity and strength to the sheet of lino, but such mounting tends to put the price of lino beyond a reasonable level. One can of course mount one's own lino. For purposes of experiment it is best to buy or cut several small pieces of unmounted lino with the intention of

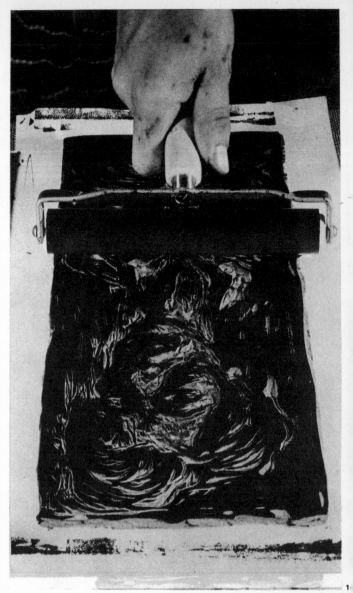

148

1

mounting them should the designs cut into them prove satisfactory, for there is little point in going to the trouble and expense of a mount until one is sure that the design will be worth printing.

The simplest tool for cutting away the linoleum surface is a sharp penknife, but there are a variety of lino tools for sale which are especially made for the job and are more easily handled. Only three or four cutting shapes are really necessary: two sizes of V shaped cutters, one semi-circular shape and a sharp cutting blade. All these cutting tools are made so as to interchange with a common handle. The lino block is not so sensitive a surface that the nature of the tool will effect to any important extent the quality of the design on it: one tool, the small V-shaped one, is all that is required for the majority of designs. The portrait print on plate 152 was cut with such a tool and printed, in spite of its large size, without a mounting.

The paper and ink used for lino printing depends entirely on the taste of the artist. A thick paper tends to be more durable, a thin paper more receptive. A damp Japanese printing paper is by far the best to use for a final print, but almost any paper without a pronounced grain is suitable, provided it has been well dampened. The best method of preparing damp paper is to wet one or two sheets of blotting paper and interleave one sheet of dry printing paper with one sheet of wet blotting paper and leave a pile of it under pressure for a few hours, beneath a weight of heavy books or in a press. Alternatively, one can damp the paper with a sponge before printing. A thick oil-bound printer's ink is very good for printing onto undampened paper, but it is a slow drier. Water paint can give fine results also, provided that the paper is dampened to the right degree. Whichever of these two inks you prefer, you must remember that a roller which has been used for oil-printing for any length of time does not take readily to water-bound inks.

Cutting into the block of lino should be preceded by much thought and deliberation. The usual advice to beginners, is that they should make one or two experimental cuts onto a piece of lino in order to catch the 'feel' of it, but there is no reason why one should not tackle the business of producing a design right from the start. You

hould, however, be careful to choose a simple design for
our first effort, and this design should be already made
on a piece of paper before you attempt to draw it out on
he sheet of lino. You must remember that the white parts
of your design are to be cut away on the block, and that
t is very difficult to obtain very fine lines on a lino block.
ry to think of your design in terms of flat areas of black
nd white, and handle the design in a bold, direct manner.

A simple way of transferring a design to the lino block
s to paint the lino surface with a thin coat of white poster
aint and allow it to dry. If you trace your design onto
ne tracing paper and then place this pencil-side down
nto the white lino and rub over its back with a few firm
encil strikes you will find that a clear pencil outline has
een transferred to the white surface. This traced outline
ill quite naturally be in reverse to your original drawing,
nd this is exactly what is required for when your block is
nally printed it will also come out in reverse. Thus, if the
esign is transferred to the block in reverse, it will be
rinted the 'right way round' in the final printing stage.

Once you have transferred your design to the lino you

152 Lino cut, Fred Gettings. Author's collection

153-
156 Steps in making a card print

157 Card print, Fred Gettings. Author's collection

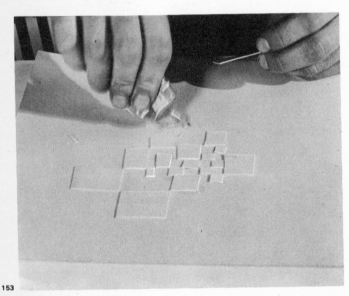

153

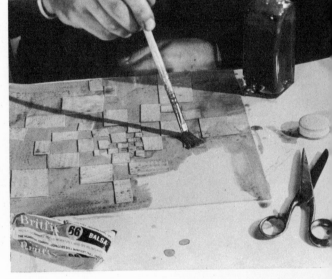

can begin to cut away the areas you wish to appear white on your print, leaving those parts of your design which are black on your original design as raised lino. The V-shaped cutting tool is the easiest to handle in the beginning stages. It should be pushed firmly, never towards your body in case it should slip, and not too deeply, so as to remove a fairly even strip of lino and leave a neat groove in the block which will print as a white line. This tool, besides being useful for sketching out the first general outlines of the pattern, may be used for a variety of textures in the form of triangular pecks into the lino surface, and also for cross hatching, provided this is not done too deeply. The semi-circular gouge is best employed in cleaning large areas of lino away. It is advisable not to dig too deeply with this tool as it tends to lift out uneven areas of lino surface as it is pushed along. The lino knife or penknife is really a one-sided V-shaped tool, and to obtain any line for printing it is necessary to make two cuts at angles to each other. In this way it is possible to cut a white line with a considerably richer appearance than with a V-shaped tool.

Most books on elementary lino-cutting suggest that the beginner should think of his design in terms of flat blocks and large masses of shapes – presumably because the lino surface is not adapted to detailed cutting. I feel, however, that this is not sound advice. Large areas of black and white will lend a solidity to the design, but this approach to lino cutting in which one thinks in terms of flat masses of black and white all too often results in a turgid, uninteresting balance of unrelated forms. It is far better to think of your design in terms of the cutting tools you are using. In my opinion a good lino cut will show evidence of the way the cutting tool has been manipulated. If you examine the portrait at plate 152 you will see that the design is built out of clear and simple strokes of the cutting tool, and that any balance of large masses is a result of this cutting technique.

I have often seen beginners, who have not quite grasped the principles of lino-cutting, smoothing off the cut out area of lino, and even cutting right through the lino to the string netting at its base. Neither of these practices are necessary to make a good print: indeed they are even

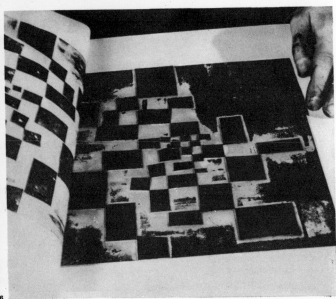

157

harmful as they tend to weaken the structure of the lino sheet and to render a mounting block essential. A cut of about an eighth of an inch is quite sufficient, and a quarter of an inch slightly too much. When removing large expanses of lino it is a good thing to allow small pieces of the lino to remain with their surface intact. These will print as small areas of texture, and besides often looking rather pleasant they have the effect of preserving the lino structure. If such textures do mar the design then they can always be removed later.

After a certain amount of work has been done on the block, so that most of the design is incorporated in the cuts, it will be advisable to take a 'proof' print to see how the work is progressing.

Roll a plentiful supply of ink onto a sheet of glass with a fairly large roller, and then apply a coating of ink to the surface of the lino. Take care not to lift the roller until it has travelled across the whole extent of your block, and make sure that there is an even deposit of ink over the whole of the raised surface by rolling in different directions. Now take a piece of dampened paper and after

blotting its surface carefully, place it face down onto your printing block. Now smooth down the paper over the block with your thumb until you are sure that there are no cockles in the paper. You may now begin to burnish the print with the back of a tablespoon, as in plate 149. After you are sure that you have burnished over the whole extent of the printing surface, lift one corner of the paper and see what the quality of your print is like (plate 150). If you are satisfied strip it off completely from the block. If you have used damp paper for the printing, pin the proof onto a piece of board with four drawing pins to prevent it from curling or cockling whilst it dries.

You may now use this proof print as a guide for further cutting, and work at your lino block until you have achieved the result you seek.

The lovely print *Heron* by thirteen-year-old Tony Donnelly (plate 158) was made by overprinting successive lino blocks in three separate colours.

Instead of cutting into a surface in order to obtain a relief, it is possible to *add* a thin raised surface to a base and to take prints from this.

The easiest method of incorporating this principle is to stick pieces of card onto a large sheet of strong card, strawboard or hardboard, so that whatever shapes are stuck down will print in reverse. For experimental purposes by far the simplest thing to do is to cut out a lot of squares and oblongs of different sizes from a sheet of thin cardboard and to stick them down with glue as shown in plate 153. Allow the glue to dry, preferably under pressure beneath a pile of books or in a nipping press, and then paint the whole of the printing face with a thin coat of shellac (sometimes known as 'knotting') so as to make the surface non-absorbent and easy to print. As soon as the shellac is quite dry you can roll the surface with ink and print by spoon rubbing in much the same way as you did for lino printing.

As you can see from a specimen print on plate 157, if the relief is not very high, the ink will be rolled onto the base as well as the relief and will print as a background texture. This does not matter a great deal – particularly when you are printing an abstract design of squares like the one illustrated – but there are several ways of getting round this difficulty. You can use thick card for building your relief, that when rolled, the ink does not touch the low background (though, of course, thick card does not lend itself to delicate work), or you can wipe off the offending areas with a clean rag, although this not only takes time and permits the ink to dry into the block, but invariably the rag catches on the legitimate printing area and thus mars the print. It is possible to cut away any large expanse of background provided it is not so large as to weaken the structure of the block as a whole, and certainly you can cut the outer shape of the background to fit the silhouette of your design unless you want the shadow of a square background left, as at plate 160.

When you have printed one or two of your designs of squares you can branch out in two directions. You may try building a 'realistic' picture of cut-out shapes – trying, for example, to make a formal design within the limitations of this printing method rather like the print of a racehorse on plate 161. But in addition to experimenting with the formal aspects of your design you can experiment with the medium itself. Try out the printing possibilities of

158 'Heron'. print by Tony Donnelly, aged 13. Reproduced by courtesy of the Sunday Mirror

159 'Standing Figure', card print by Anne Davis, aged 10. Author's collection

160 'Christmas Tree' by Janet Reed, aged 9. Author's collection

161 'Racehorse' by Kim Warren, aged 8. Author's collection

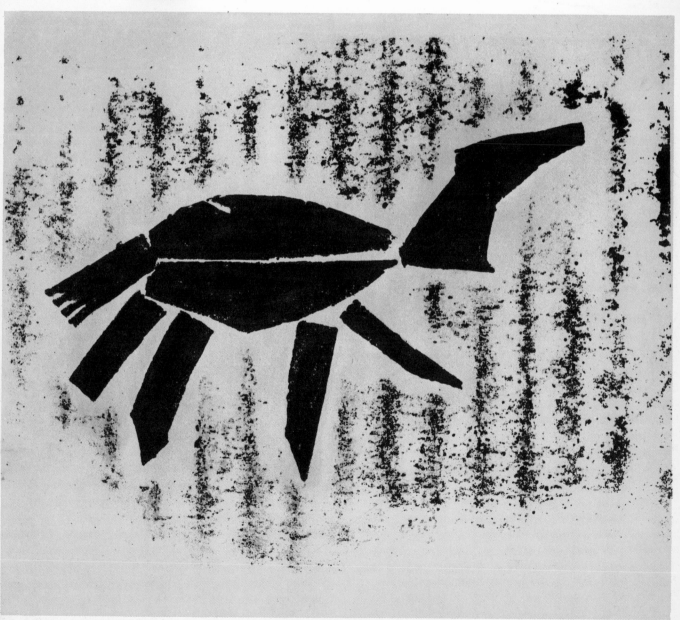

162 Fred Gettings, 'Abstract Glitter-print'

163-
165 Steps in making a Glitter-print

166 Fred Gettings, 'Glitter-print based on cave drawing'. Author's collection

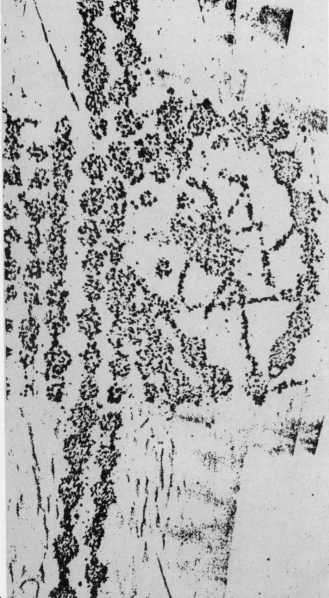

162

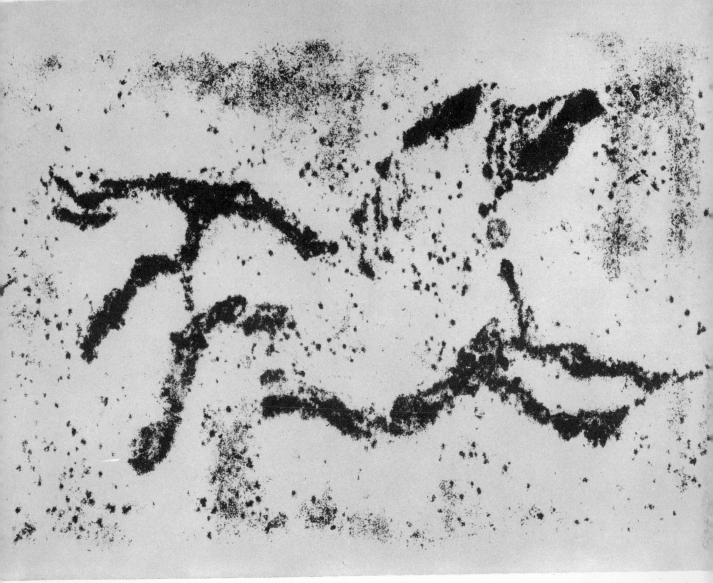

various flat objects of different thicknesses, like scraps of newspaper, matches, pieces of string etc. Try to limit yourself in the first instance by producing a picture entirely from match-sticks.

Another method of building up a relief for printing is almost a logical development of the previous one, and consists of laying a shallow wall of a powdery substance such as sawdust and cementing it with glue.

The procedure is to draw in glue directly onto a sheet of card, using the nozzle of the glue-tube as a sort of pencil, as in plate 163. For the sake of accuracy and speed (as glue dries very quickly on the card) it is a good policy to have sketched in pencil the design you wish to print. Plate 165 is a free copy of a cave painting of a running horse.

As soon as you have finished drawing, and before the glue is dry, you spread a covering of sawdust or some similar substance over the whole of the design. The dust in the illustration on plate 164 is 'star-dust glitter' which is normally used for Christmas decorations, and which is even more suitable for this kind of printing than sawdust. Allow the glue two or three hours to dry, and then brush off the

dust or glitter, and you will find that a residue has been left in the form of a wall of dust and glue (plate 165).

There are two ways of printing this kind of design. You can either print in reverse after painting a skin of shellac over its surface as in the two previous methods (taking care not to destroy the wall when rubbing with the spoon), or you can print directly by running a charged roller backwards and forwards over a piece of thin paper laid over the design. The accidental textures around the horse in plate 166 are remarkably evocative of the textures found in prehistoric cave painting, and for this reason they were allowed to stay after the initial proofing. (They could, of course, have been removed from the block by blowing onto them, or picking them off with a knife point.)

Potato printing is the simplest and best known of all relief methods. A large potato is cut in half and the smooth surface of one half is gouged into with a knife to leave a raised pattern. The potato must be left for an hour or two for the moisture to evaporate before printing, and then it is pressed onto a layer of ink which has been rolled onto a sheet of glass. The potato is printed by pressing its inked surface

167

168

onto paper. Because the substance of the potato is largely water it is only possible to print with a water-bound ink or with watercolour. The lovely picture *Warm and Cool Colours* on plate 169 was made by overprinting in thick watercolours onto a grey paper with simple potato relief squares.

Intaglio printing is, as we have already noted, a process by which ink is retained in grooves cut into a plate and transferred to the paper under immense pressure. Quite obviously it is not possible to use a printing surface which will be crushed under pressure, so in most instances intaglio printing is done from metal sheets. The best known intaglio processes are line engraving, etching in its various forms, and dry point etching. Line engraving is the oldest of these processes and consists, as its name implies, of engraving into a metal plate with a sharp V-shaped graver, but it is perhaps the most difficult, for considerable ability is required to draw with any precision into smooth metal.

Dry point etching is by far the simplest process since it consists of working into the metal plate with a sharp point. This may sound to be exactly the same as line engraving, but in fact the difference, both in technique and end

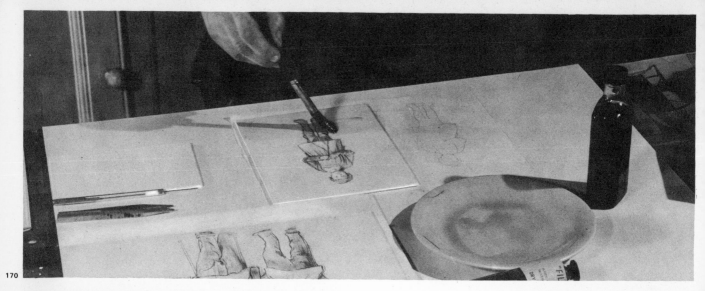

170

171

product is considerable. Whereas in line engraving the aim is to achieve a clean line with a burin, as the cutting tool is called, in dry point work the aim is to achieve a scratched line with a furrow of metal shavings along each side of the line. Whereas line engraving will print at its best as clean black line, a dry point etching will print with a unique richness of line as a result of the burr. Of course, under the tremendous pressure required for intaglio printing the metal shavings are quickly crushed, and the richness of a dry point is soon lost. For this reason dry point etchings of any quality are always limited to relatively few editions. One can do no better than spend an hour browsing through the engravings of Dürer and the dry points of Rembrandt, for both these artists are masters of these two printing methods.

The commonest form of intaglio printing nowadays is etching. This is a process which, like dry point etching, involves engraving a metal plate with fine lines into which ink is pressed and then forced out into the paper. However, the process is slightly complicated by the fact that in pure etching the lines are not directly engraved into the plate, but are bitten in with acid. This is done by covering the plate, which is usually copper, with a resin ground which is impervious to acid, and then scratching the drawing into this ground with a needle. When the drawing is completed, or a 'proof' is required, the plate, which has been protected on its back and sides with an acid resist is submerged in a bath of acid. The acid bites into the areas and lines on the plate which have been exposed through the resin by the needle. The 'etched' lines are printed by rolling ink over the whole surface of the plate and rubbing it firmly into the lines, and then wiping off the surplus ink from the surface so that the ink is contained in the channels engraved in the plate.

A reversed print of the etching is made by passing a piece of dampened paper and the inked plate through a special press. The considerable pressure of the etching press forces the damp paper into the channels so that it picks up the ink and registers the reversed print.

Etching demands much preparation, considerable equipment and a special heavy press, and it is therefore not a practical craft for the amateur artist. In recent years, however, a printing method has been introduced which brings a kind of 'dry point' etching well within the scope of the amateur. This is the 'Filmetch Process' which is similar in many respects to dry point etching but which is an intaglio process with characteristics of its own. As a method it dispenses with all the expensive equipment usually associated with intaglio printing, such as metal plates and heavy presses, and for this reason alone it could become quite popular as a process.

In the Filmetch process the metal plate is replaced by a specially prepared non-porous base such as hardboard or linoleum, which may be engraved in much the same way as a dry point etching. Although the printing is done in much the same way as in ordinary etching, there is no need for a heavy pressure, and good printing results can be obtained with an ordinary nipping press.

All the necessary materials for Filmetching can be obtained from Dryad's Ltd, but the only thing which one cannot make for oneself is the plastic and solvent which are used to prepare the 'plate'.

The plate can be made from almost any semi-porous sheeting, like hardboard. It is prepared by painting it with a coat of white cellulose paint which serves the dual purpose of presenting a good adhesive surface for the application of plastic, and of allowing the preparatory pencil drawing to show up clearly.

As the final print will be in reverse it is advisable to make a direct tracing of the drawing you wish to print and then transfer this to the prepared plate by placing it face down over the plate and impregnating the graphite onto the white surface by running a pencil firmly over the back of the tracing. One may work directly onto a plate without any preparatory drawing, in which case one should move directly onto the next stage of giving the plate a coating of plastic.

The plastic for Filmetching is supplied in a tube, and its solvent in a small bottle. Equal amounts of plastic and solvent should be mixed into a saucer for a sufficient time to allow all the numerous small bubbles to disappear. The plastic should be just about thick enough to brush onto the plate easily. As it is transparent the pencil drawing already on the sheet will show through very clearly. The plastic tends to set to a jelly in just over half an hour, so one should not mix more than an amount sufficient to prepare the

173

number of plates one intends to work within the next few hours.

The plastic should be brushed liberally onto the prepared plate with a large brush, and then the plate should be placed under cover in a horizontal position for a while so that the tacky plastic does not pick up too much dust from the atmosphere. The plate should take about half an hour to dry, but this time will vary with the nature of the plastic mixture. In any event one should not leave the plate too long before needling into it, otherwise its surface will become intractable.

The drawing into the plastic is done with a needle which may be purchased with the Filmetch material or made at home. The needle used in plate 171 was made by fixing an ordinary sewing needle into a length of glass tubing with sealing wax. The plate should be held in such a position that the light enables one to see clearly the 'biting' action of the needle as one works into the plastic surface so that one may distinguish the etched line from the pencil line already on the plate. The particles of plastic which are thrown up by the needle should be dusted off frequently with a rag, and if the line should furrow unevenly at the sides, or if it should drag and retain particles in its wake, the plastic surface is not ready for etching.

As the plastic surface grows harder it will resist the needle point more and more, and it will become increasingly difficult to bite deeply into the surface. If the surface should become impossibly hard it may be softened up a little with a careful application of the solvent, but this is not a step to be recommended, being generally messy and destructive to those lines which are already drawn to satisfaction. The surface of the plate, in part or in localised areas, may be re-prepared with a coating of plastic ready for re-working, but in principle one should aim at finishing the plate in one go.

The surface of the plate must be allowed to set quite hard before printing is attempted. A week is the ideal time, and a minimum of three days must be allowed otherwise the surface of the plastic may be ruined in the press. The hardness of the surface is directly related to the number of prints which may be obtained from the plate, so the longer it is left the better. Once the plate is dried it may be used many times, and it does not deteriorate with the passing of time.

The best paper for printing is a substantially heavy cartridge, but as different paper surfaces and qualities give different results only experiment will show the particular paper most suitable for one's own type of drawing. As the paper tissue has to be forced into the fine lines on the engraved plastic surface, it must be thoroughly dampened before use. Each sheet of printing paper must be a few inches larger than the plate to allow for handling and mounting.

A quantity of black letterpress ink must be mixed with half as much thinners and rolled or dabbed onto the plate so that all the lines are filled with ink. The surface of the plate should then be wiped clean with a piece of rag and polished clean with rapid but firm flicks of a smooth cloth so that no ink remains on the surface and as much as possible is held in the engraved channels. The ink charged lines will now show up clearly against the white base.

The actual printing is done by placing a dampened sheet of printing paper over the plate and placing these on a bed of waste paper in a nipping press with the inked plate surface upwards. Over the back of the printing paper there should be a sheet of blotting paper and a wad of waste paper. The nipping press should be screwed down as tightly as possible and left for a few minutes before the plate and print are removed for examination. As the wet paper will tend to buckle as it dries one should choose the best prints and stick these down on a drawing board with a piece of sellotape or drawing pins until quite dry.

If the plate is not cleaned thoroughly the thin lines of the drawing will tend to fill up and their printing power will be diminished. When a sufficient number of prints have been taken the plate should be washed over with paraffin, and one or two proofs taken to remove all traces of ink from the channels.

Texture Pictures

So far we have tended to regard texture only in terms of its being useful for 'filling in' line drawings, or as an end product of various printing techniques. This must not blind us to the fact that texture may be used in its own right to produce very satisfactory designs. To some extent we have already seen this in *People entering the gates of a Tube* on plate 142.

Good texture work demands that one should be prepared to experiment with many methods of obtaining texture. This is best done in the initial stages by restricting oneself to one colour, such as black, and one medium, such as Indian ink.

The most obvious way of making a texture is by splatter work (plate 174). An old toothbrush with fairly resilient bristles, a paint brush and a knife are the only materials you will require besides the ink and paper. If you brush the ink onto the toothbrush bristles with a paint brush there will be less chance of the ink dropping all over your drawing as you splatter, which is what it does when the whole of the toothbrush is dipped into the ink. Once you have placed a good supply of ink on the toothbrush, run the edge of the knife lightly across the top of the bristles and they will spring back and throw a fine spray of ink in the opposite direction to the knife movement. The kinds of textures you can obtain in this way are various – there will be quite a different texture if you spray almost horizontally to the paper, for example, than if you spray vertically to it. The speed with which you pull back the knife will vary the texture, as will the consistency of the ink.

You can spray round cut-out shapes in order to leave a pattern on the paper, or you can spray directly onto the paper and then quickly do a drawing with a match-stick whilst the ink is still wet. If you splatter over cut-out shapes be careful to allow the ink to dry completely before you lift the shape off the paper otherwise you will drag the ink along the edge of the shape and ruin its silhouette.

An interesting effect can be achieved by taking three sheets of paper all of the same size and cutting out of them simple patterns of an abstract nature. You then place one of them over a sheet of clean paper and splatter the design. When it is dry you remove it and place over the same sheet the second cut-out paper and splatter that. You will now have the two patterns on the paper, and where the patterns

174 Fred Gettings, 'Homage to Prampolini'. Author's collection

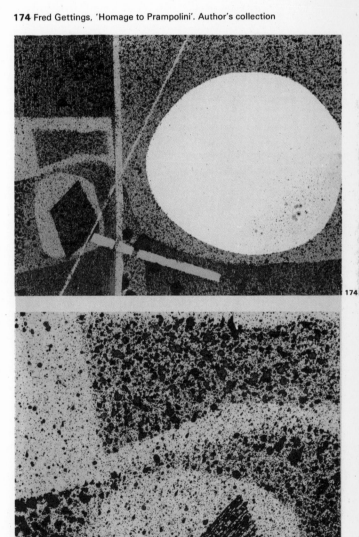

174

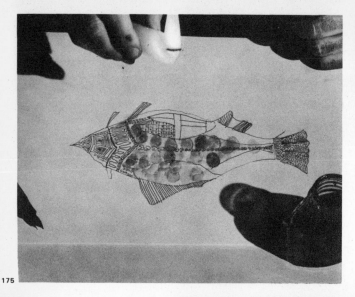

175

1

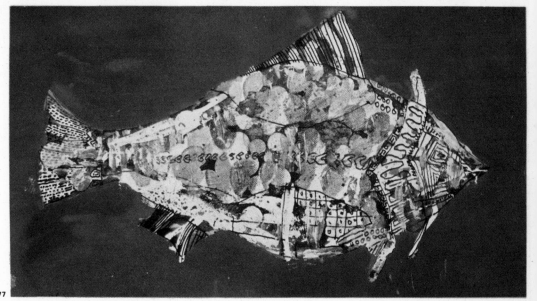

177

overlapped the paper will have been splattered twice. If you repeat the process with the third shape you will have some areas which have been splattered three times, some twice, some once and some not at all. You could, of course, use different colours for each splatter process.

Candle wax may be used to good textural effect. The wax may be dropped directly onto the paper by holding a lighted candle above a drawing and allowing blobs of wax to fall onto it, or it may be smeared on by drawing with a candle onto the sheet.

The texture in both cases results from the property the wax has of repelling ink.

A useful exercise is to take a simple line drawing, like the one on plate 175, and add textures and nuances of colour step by step until a satisfactory picture has been produced. First of all drop hot wax onto the drawing (see plate 175). Observe that the drawing was given a finger-print texture before the wax was applied. You can smear wax onto the picture where necessary, and then run a wash of water colour or ink completely over the drawing. The waxed areas will reject the ink and leave a very interesting texture. The

wax may be scraped off with a knife, and if the picture is still not satisfactory you can repeat the process entirely, or simply brush over another thin wash of colour. The paper surface will not be very receptive to water paints, but it will be possible to add splashes of oil paint or even very viscous water colour or gouache direct from the tube. In the final design on plate 177 smears of white oil-paint have been added.

Constructing an abstract picture out of textural elements is one of the most exciting ways of painting. Start out with a blank sheet of paper and try to have no idea in your mind of the sort of design you are about to produce, and let the picture work itself out as you go along. Perhaps you could start with a few circular smears, like the ones in plate 182: these are produced by taking a ball of crumpled paper and pressing it down into a film of ink rolled on glass and then 'printing' it onto the paper by twisting it down with a circular motion of the wrist. Your next step may be to cover a few areas of the paper with an inked roller. You might then draw onto the painting with a candle and then run a wash of colour over it. If your picture is not quite satisfactory you

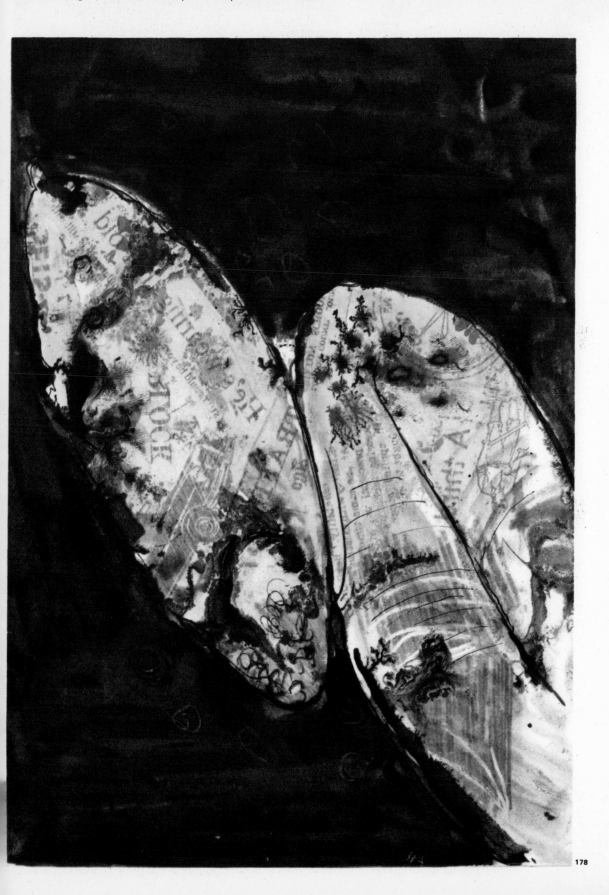

178

179

180

181

could splatter over it with a spray of thick blobs of paint or add textures in oil-paint over the top. The aim of the exercise is to continue adding textures to a paper in an inventive way until a satisfactory picture has been achieved. An interesting 'printed' texture can be obtained by rubbing the back of a waxed sheet of paper onto a piece of newsprint. The wax surface actually picks up some of the ink from the printed newspaper, leaving a reversed copy on the waxed paper. The sepia painting *Slow Rotation* on plate 174, was wax printed with reversed newsprint. The hotch-potch of lettering above the texture crowd movement in plate 142 was obtained in this way. Rauschenberg, the contemporary American artist, has used this wax printing a great deal in his work – particularly in his illustrations to Danté.

Children and Chalked Wall by Joan Eardley admirably demonstrates how textures may be incorporated into a realistic composition of the dècorative type. The wall texture has been built up from bits of newspaper, scumbling of pigment and painted or stencilled words. Some of the words are actually taken from newsprint.

179-
181 Texture Painting

182-
183 Texture prints made from screwed-up ball of paper

184 Joan Eardley, 'Children and Chalked Wall'. By courtesy of Roland, Browse and Delbanco

Collage

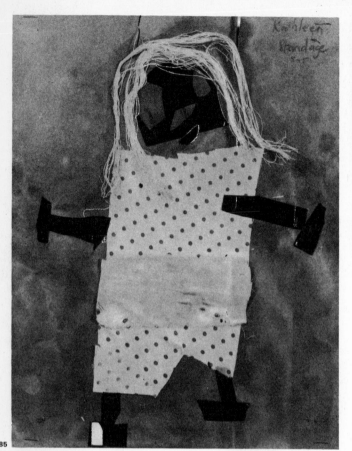

185 'Ready for Bed' by Kathleen Standage, aged 5. Milford Infants' School, Lincolnshire

186 'White Stallion' by Angela Smith, aged 7. Rathfern Junior Mixed School, London, S.E.6.

187 Schwitters, 'The Neatest Trick of the Month'. Collection of Richard S. Zeisler, New York

The texture work in the background of Joan Eardley's painting on plate 184 may be described as 'collage'. The word collage is derived from the French word for glue, and is applied to that art form which is supposed to have been developed by the early Cubists. The art of collage consists of sticking down scraps of waste paper, fabric and other odds and ends to form a decorative surface which may or may not carry some meaning in a symbolical or directly illustrative way. The Victorians often decorated fire screens and room dividers with scrap cuttings from Christmas cards and magazines in a way which resembles collage, so that art form could hardly be said to have been 'invented' by the Cubists at all.

Several artists I know have spent many hours constructing immense collages on their studio walls instead of decorating them in the normal way. With a collection of newspaper and magazine cuttings you can spend many profitable hours constructing such collages, either on a large scale, as a mural, or on a small scale as individual pictures. The German artist Schwitters, who was one of the greatest of collage builders, constructed the interior of his house

in Hanover as one immense and complicated collage. Schwitters termed his collage *Merz*, a meaningless word derived from the last four letters of *kommerz* which remained on a fragment of newspaper he was sticking onto one of his collages. Each room in his house was made into a complex, labyrinthine system of geometric and two-dimensional constructions. His *Merz* house, as he called it, was razed to the ground by bombs in the last war. Schwitters' lovely collage *The Neatest Trick of the Month* on plate 187 is built out of newspapers, bus tickets, photographs and waste crumpled tissue. He was fond of choosing his titles from the fragmentary words and captions which were left on his collage. His collage work has no deep significance: they are beautiful arrangements of texture, shapes and colours in the decorative tradition.

There are basically three ways of tackling the problem of collage. You can aim simply at producing the sort of collage which Schwitters would construct, and finish up with an abstract arrangement of colours and shapes. You could make pictures from cut-outs of realistic drawings or photographs merged together to convey a very definite meaning

or idea (you have already touched on this type of collage in basic design, when you were experimenting with cut-outs of cricketers), or you could follow the technique practised by Dubuffet and, with the aid of torn or cut out pieces of paper, construct a realistic picture.

The first method presents its own specific problems. Each extra piece of paper you stick onto the main sheet will change the relationship of the whole picture, as you will have learned from your basic design studies. The main difficulty is knowing when to stop: not knowing how to gauge the exact moment when to stick another piece of paper or string down will ruin the collage. A simple exercise which will teach you a great deal about the art of collage in particular and about composition as a whole is to accept a certain discipline before you undertake the actual collage. You can, for example, take a piece of newspaper ten by eight inches as the basic working sheet, and only eight pieces of scrap from which to construct a pleasant ensemble. Each of the eight pieces must be laid out before you, and you must stick them down one by one, making no alteration to any which have already been stuck down. Each time you

stick down one of the pieces a 'new' composition will result which must then be amended or corrected by the next piece until the total scraps allotted for your picture are used. The best practical advice which can be given in relation to this type of abstract collage is 'look at the work of Schwitters'. You must not be afraid of experimenting for yourself – a few judiciously placed pencil lines often improve a drab or lifeless collage.

The second method of collage is very difficult indeed. To use odd scraps and cut-outs to convey some meaning is not very easy, and it is a help to dismiss the problems of colour for some time by restricting oneself to black and white montage. The best photographs for this type of work are often found in scientific magazines, but the type of cut-outs you select will, of course, depend on what sort of meaning you wish to convey. An excellent experiment is to select a title before you even begin to choose your cut-outs, and then try to find the ones which will best express the idea behind your title.

The third method of collage is the most fascinating. It may be as simple in approach as the lovely picture by seven-

188

year-old Angela Smith at plate 186, which is really a sort of paper mosaic, or as simple as the picture by five-year-old Kathleen Standage *Ready for Bed,* which is made out of cloth, cotton and sticky paper, or it may be as refined as the colourful *Tree* collage (plate 189), which was made by sticking bits of cut up cereal packet onto a strawboard.

Another simple exercise you might care to undertake is to make a collage by building up a picture from strips of newspaper and sticking them onto a black background, like the chair in plate 120.

The point where a collage turns into a painting is very hard to determine. When, in the early days of Cubism round about 1912, Braque and Picasso started to stick pieces of newspaper onto their canvas as an integral part of their painting, they initiated a movement which has slowly evolved into a new form of art sometimes referred to as 'the art of assemblage'. Since these early days, collage of scraps of paper has been superseded by collage of scraps of metal, bits of sacking and almost anything the artist can lay his hands on. One artist stuck a lot of forks and spoons onto a glass-covered box and called it *Arteriosclerosis,* whilst another

artist stuck down a toy pistol, a piece of rope and steel gear onto a sheet of painted plywood and called it *Tu est moi.* This sort of 'painting' is really an extended form of collage, and in many cases it is not directed towards beauty, but consists of a sort of revolt at existing canons of art. One artist friend of mine has said to me 'I can't bear even the smell of paint: give me old tin cans any day!'

One way of making an assemblage painting is to stick down pieces of sacking onto a board. The very beautiful *Fish on Table* by Anne Barren was made out of sacking. The fish itself is a piece of rolled up hessian stained with oil paint, and its eye is the top of a paint tube glued onto the sacking. The beauty of this picture stems primarily from the lovely colour and texture, but one very important element is the simple structure of the table top echoing the shape and proportion of the picture.

A much more sophisticated 'assemblage' is Tilson's construction at plate 190, which is built out of squares of wood. Here again an important element is the slab-like structure of the assemblage and the beautiful colours of the natural wood surface.

The Found Object

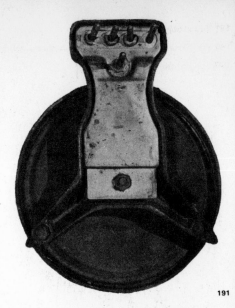

In the early part of this century the French painter Marcel Duchamp conceived the idea of the 'readymade'. A readymade is an object which exists in its own right and usually for some functional purpose, like a bottle rack or a smoothing iron, which the artist divorces from its usual context and, without making any alteration to it, exhibits it as a work of art. Duchamp would have considered the gin trap (plate 193) a 'readymade' because it has been placed 'on show' on my studio wall instead of being used for the purpose for which it was intended. The creative effort involved in producing a readymade work of art rests purely on the *choice* of the object, and has nothing to do with the object itself. The choice an artist makes is a reflection of himself.

As one might expect, there was a strong reaction to Duchamp's idea of 'readymade' art – and this in spite of the fact that archaeological research has shown that 'readymades' in the form of smooth pebbles and stones shaped like animals were probably the earliest 'art' form. Most people missed the force of Duchamp's argument, which was that *choice* of an object, rather like the choice of a new suit, is a creative act in which the personality and understanding of the artist is given its full expression. They also failed to understand his idea that an object need not be created by an artist to be worthy of 'aesthetic' appreciation. To a certain extent Duchamp's art, like most good creative art, was in revolt at existing canons of taste, and was even termed 'anti-art' by its protagonists; but it was also coloured by a vital sense of humour.

One of Duchamp's close friends, Man Ray, constructed a work entitled *Gift* which was nothing but a flat-iron studded on the smooth side with tacks. Such humour was considered by most people to be 'in bad taste', particularly when Duchamp suggested the idea of 'reciprocal readymades' which were works of art used functionally – like using a Rembrandt painting as an ironing board. When Duchamp sent an inverted urinal signed 'R. Mutt, 1917' to an exhibition in New York matters really came to a head. Duchamp felt himself called upon to defend his 'work of art', and he dismissed the selection committee's charge that the urinal was 'immoral and vulgar' with the observation that a urinal is no more immoral than a bath tub, and he pointed out

that it was a fixture that you can see every day in a plumber's show window. To the selector's claims that the work was plagiaristic, being a simple piece of plumbing, Duchamp replied that the *Fountain*, as he called it, had been made by Richard Mutt, who was a manufacturer of sanitary hardware. His defence of the *Fountain* stands as a defence of all readymade art:

Whether Mr Mutt with his own hands made the fountain or not has no importance. He CHOSE it. He took an ordinary article of life, placed it so that its useful significance disappeared under the new title and point of view – created a new thought for that object.

The point of Duchamp's argument is still with us. The creative act is not solely a matter of an artist-spectator relationship, but one of a personal reaction to external objects. What Duchamp was saying in lengthy and perhaps jocular terms was that the recognition and enjoyment of a work of art or any object is as much a creative act as the production of the work itself.

Duchamp's efforts led to the popularisation of a new 'art form' in which *found objects,* such as pieces of rotting wood, corkscrews, dustbin lids and even stones were considered to have aesthetic possibilities and exhibited. A 'found object' differs from a readymade in that a readymade is a functional thing divorced from its usual background and thereby rendered useless, whereas a found object is something which is interesting or beautiful and which is exhibited purely because of these qualities. There is no strict division between these two art forms, however. The gin trap at plate 193 is in one sense a 'found object' exhibited for its abstract form, its lovely colour and its texture; but because it is exhibited (as in the photograph) with its spring set to catch some creature, it is in this sense a 'readymade'. Its function is to trap, yet it has been placed in the very position where it cannot catch anything – on a vertical wall. As with all 'readymades' there is an underlying humour in its creation. The rusty object at plate 191, which was taken from an old electric oven, is not of the dual nature: it is simply a found object.

We have all at one time or another indulged in 'found object' art, as we have all collected sea shells, coloured pebbles and strangely shaped stones because of their beauty

191 Found object

192 Fred Gettings, 'Whimsical Figure'. Author's collection

193 Set gin trap

192

193

194

194 Fred Gettings, 'War Bird'. Author's collection

195 Fred Gettings, 'K'. Author's collection

196 Fred Gettings, 'Homage to Kafka'. Author's collection

195

196

or interest. The impulse to collect these objects, to *choose* them from all other objects, springs from a deep creative urge which is at least as old as the earliest man. Consideration of the creative aspect of this kind of art form will lead to an understanding of how art may be defined in terms of choice of action.

There is one development on the art of the readymade and the found object which will be of interest to us in that we can utilise it in our search for expression. This art form is sometimes called 'Found Object Composed' and is related directly to collage. The idea of this form of expression is that some readymade or found object is altered slightly so as to change its original significance and to transform it into a new thing. We can take some old and disused object, 'an ordinary article of life', as Duchamp put it, and by adding other found objects, transform it.

The *War Bird* on plate 194 is quite obviously made from an old fire grate, but it has none-the-less a compelling individuality of its own. The creative act involved in making the *War Bird* lay first of all in realising the potentiality of the old grate. Even without the addition of the eyes and

beak it looked sufficiently like a peacock to suggest both a bird and pride. The choice of the two nut heads for eyes and a rusty nail for beak was a fairly simple matter, but there was much deliberation on the size of the beak before the present one was adopted. The rusting process was a choice based on experience – the knowledge that rusted iron can look very beautiful. The *War Bird* was hung in a trough of dirty water for several weeks until the daily examination revealed that the desired effect of colour and texture had been obtained. Choice of title was in itself a creative act – 'peacock' and 'pride' suggested arrogance, whilst the mechanical symmetry of shape somehow suggested the mechanicalness of warfare. When fixed on as a beak the nail looked cruel, even predatory, and the whole 'bird' had an appearance of an antiquated instrument of torture. The next step from these associations to its title was comparatively easy.

The attempt to imbue the grate with a new life without hiding its identity went through many stages. At one point the centre rung of iron was studded with an orderly row of screws and nails which were intended to suggest a forward

197

197 Fred Gettings, 'Mask'. Author's collection

198 Fred Gettings, 'Lock Bridge'. Collection of Mr. and Mrs. Colin Richmond

aggressive movement, so that the whole object evoked an image of some strange and ancient 'deterrent', but another transformation called for the complete removal of the sliding front unit of the grate which was invested with a face made from twisted wire.

The *War Bird* may undergo many such transformations yet: an artist's attitude to a work of art should never be final. A work of art is created anew each time it is looked at, so there is no reason why it should not be continually changed by its creator.

A good exercise is to take an object like an old can or a pair of scissors, and attempt to transform it with the minimum of trimmings. Picasso brought together two related found objects to make a magnificent bull's head: from a saddle and a pair of handle-bars from a bicycle. In this work of art neither the handlebar nor the saddle loses its identity yet they both contribute to producing a most startling presence. The effort involved in creating the head was minimal, and this is one of the criteria in the art of 'Found Object Composed'.

For this sort of activity one needs to establish a collection

of old waste metal and bric-à-brac. The wider one's collection, the wider one's creative scope. Old clocks and watches provide invaluable material for this kind of work – both *Whimsical Figure* (plate 192) and the figure *K* in plate 195 were constructed from parts out of a broken clock.

It is interesting to see how *K* was incorporated into a new assemblage just after the photograph had been taken. My aim with *K* was to create a 'hero' bewildered by life, and I felt after making the figure that the bewilderment could best be expressed if *K* were placed against a background which would reduce his stature. The ideal background was the rusty seed spreader in plate 196 which resembled a castle turret and reminded me of Kafka's novel *The Castle*. When I had placed *K* against the background and fastened him down with Araldite and nuts and bolts I was quite satisfied with the result and christened the whole assemblage *Homage to Kafka*.

Flat sheets of metal are particularly useful for building up sculpture, reliefs or pictures. The flat sheet of cast iron in plate 197 was taken from a rusty old farm vehicle, and so resembled a human face that I couldn't resist building onto

it a pair of eyes, a nose and a mouth out of nails.

The metal sheet in *The Lock Bridge* on plate 198 came from an old car front, whilst the wooden structure to the right of the picture was found on a bomb site in London. They are both fixed to the black hardboard with nails and nuts and bolts.

Work with such materials as these and along the lines of the examples given will open your eyes to the beauties of the things which are so often relegated to the scrap heap.

Plaster Technique

199

200

Few people realise what wonderful things can be made from plaster. Works of art ranging from decorative plaques for a wall or shelf to immense garden statues can be made by simple plaster techniques which are exciting to learn and very instructive to experiment with.

Our first experiment will be to make a 'print' in plasticine or clay, from a flat piece of plaster. The materials we shall need are plaster of Paris in powder form, two or three sticks of plasticine, a few modelling tools and a small sheet of glass.

Onto the sheet of glass model a fairly substantial wall of plasticine about an inch high, as in plate 200. Do not make the area too large, otherwise your final cast of plaster will be clumsy to handle and more likely to break – a good plan is to divide the large area into two or even three smaller areas, as in the picture, for in this way you will have several pieces of plaster into which you can draw. Make sure there are no gaps or weak points in the wall, especially where the plasticine rests on the glass, as you will shortly be pouring in a liquid plaster which has a habit of breaking through badly constructed walls. The walls are best made by rolling

a slab of plasticine about an inch thick and cutting off slices of the same width. If you wet the glass slightly just before you place the plasticine onto it you will find that there will be a much better union between the two.

Once you have built your walls, you can start to prepare the plaster. This is best done by adding plaster to the water rather than the reverse. Fill a basin half full of cold water, and then gently sieve into it a fine stream of plaster through your fingers, taking care to see that the plaster covers the whole of the basin bottom instead of piling up in the centre. When the bowl is nearly full, pour off the residue water until a fairly thick plaster mix is left in the bowl. At this point you must stir the mixture thoroughly, and then, with the aid of a spoon, pour it into your plasticine mould until it comes almost to the top of the walls. Put the mould aside for about two hours and wash your plaster bowl immediately.

Whilst you are waiting for your plaster slabs to dry you can prepare about eight flat pieces of plasticine which are each large enough to cover the design you wish to draw into your plaster. The best method of making these plasticine pieces is to roll a large pancake of plasticine onto a board

204

02

205

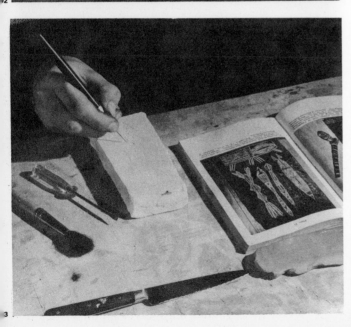

3

206

207 208 209

between two flat lengths of wood about half an inch high. When this has been rolled you can cut the plasticine to the desired size with a sharp knife. Put these eight pieces on one side when they are ready and cover them with a sheet of cloth so that chippings of plaster will not spoil them.

When the two hours have elapsed, strip away the plasticine walls from around your hard plaster and slide each block of plaster off the glass surface. You will see that the bottom of the plaster is literally glass smooth. Allow another hour for the surface to dry perfectly by contact with the air, and then smooth off the edges with a penknife, as they tend to flake when the plaster is worked.

You now have a reasonably hard smooth surface into which you can draw with a needle point (plate 203). It is possible to draw onto this surface in pencil to act as a guide for your needle, but a more satisfactory method is to transfer your drawing onto the block with tracing paper as described on page 81.

Once you have transferred the design onto the plaster block you can begin to draw into it with a sharp point. You must remember that whatever you dig out will print as a raised surface. As you progress with your drawing you will find that it is difficult to draw in a very fine line, but that the block surface lends itself well to texture. In the series of illustrations (plates 203-205) I am copying a bark drawing reproduced in the Penguin *Primitive Art*. If you choose to copy a picture from a book, as in the illustrations, you must be careful to make an effort to 'translate' the original picture into terms of the technique you are using. For example, the Australian aborigine ritual implement which so closely resembles a fish, (plate 199) was originally painted with a brush on bark. It is very easy to 'cross hatch' line when using a brush, but it is extremely difficult to do so with a needle point on plaster. You would therefore have to find some other equivalent to cross hatching on your surface. Biting into the surface with your needle, held vertical, results in a most interesting texture which could be used for this purpose. Do not stick too literally to the design you are copying. Once you have drawn in the main features of your design, close the book you are copying from and rely on your own inventive faculty for everything else. In this way you will allow the design to evolve in terms of the material

you are using instead of impressing a design proper to another technique into service.

When you have drawn into the plaster for some while you can make a 'proof' impression to see how your design is getting on. First of all brush out as much of the plaster dust from your engraving as possible, and then take one of the flat pieces of plasticine which you prepared earlier, and press it firmly into your design, as shown in plate 204. When you peel off the plasticine you will find an impression of your design on its surface. You can then place this next to your plaster slab and use it for a guide to further work on your design. No matter how carefully you brush the plaster from your cutting you will find that the plasticine will have pulled out a lot of white plaster dust. If there is a great deal of this on your plasticine you will have to throw away the pieces when you have finished using the design, as the small pieces of plaster render it useless for further modelling. To avoid waste you can cut off as much of the plaster dust as possible and then store the rest in a box for rough modelling work, like making walls for moulds.

You can work on your plaster, continually making check printings to see how your design is faring, until you are quite satisfied with what you have produced. You must then completely clean the mould of all dust by brushing it and pressing in pieces of plasticine until all the impressions are quite clean. Your mould will then be ready for clay work.

The five clay 'prints' (plates 207 to 211) were made in the above technique by young children. The method is particularly adaptable for making small pendants and earrings in clay which can be fired at a later date.

The process we have just examined consists of producing a design in plaster and then transferring this to clay or plasticine, but this procedure can be reversed with equally exciting results.

Onto a wooden board roll a sheet of plasticine about nine inches in area and about one inch thick. Into the plasticine area press any objects you can find which make an interesting pattern or surface. As you will see from the illustration at plate 212, almost any object will do: there is the impression of a small pair of scissors; a pair of calipers, a cine roll and a spring. Various textures have been made with modelling tools – to the left is a film

207 'A Lady', clay 'print' by Patricia Pitman, aged 11. Author's collection

208 'Church', clay 'print' by Pauline Crossfield, aged 6. Author's collection

209 'Abstract', clay 'print' by Leigh Warren, aged 11. Author's collection

210 'Man', clay 'print' by Anne Davis, aged 10. Author's collection

211 'Tree', clay 'print' by Briony Ensor, aged 10. Author's collection

210

211

spool, in the centre a texture made by pushing pieces of
wood into the plaster under varying pressures, in the top
left-hand corner are the interesting semi-circular patterns
left by nail heads, and at the bottom right the pattern left by
dragged match-sticks. You should try to make as many of
these different patterns on your plasticine as you can, as this
first attempt is by way of experiment before you launch out
into the job of making an actual abstract cast.

Once your plasticine surface is covered with texture you
must build a solid wall of plasticine around your design so
that you can pour in your plaster of Paris. When you mix
your plaster make it slightly more liquid than when you were
constructing your blocks on glass, as the plaster has to be
thin enough to run into the depressions you have made in
the plasticine. When you have poured a thin mixture of
plaster onto your design you must brush it lightly with a
thick soft brush to make sure that you dislodge all the air
bubbles which have been trapped by the plaster in the
delicate lines and textures on the plasticine. Do not brush
too heavily or you will mar your design with brush strokes.

When you have poured in sufficient plaster to fill the
mould leave it for about six hours before peeling off the
plasticine to examine the finished cast. You must leave this
type of cast to dry for a considerably longer time than when
you were making a flat plaster surface as the plaster in the
textured surface tends to break off rather easily until it is
set and strong enough to pull off.

You will find that certain kinds of texture lend themselves
to easy reproduction, whereas others are not at all suitable.
Plate 217 is a cast of the experimental block in plate 212.
You will see that the tips of the semi-circles which were
made by pressing in the top of the screw have been broken
off – this is because the tips, which are three dimensional
projections, trapped the plaster when the cast was made and
the portions which were trapped remained behind when the
block was removed. This type of pattern tends to be
structurally weak, and great care has to be taken with it when
casting. The two impressions made by the small springs at
the top of the cast are not at all satisfactory as little air bubbles
were left in each of the wire impressions, and we have
each of these bubbles reproduced in the form of circular
impressions. If you have made a large number of different

212-
215 Making a plaster impression
216 'Soldiers', by Stephen Grimsley, aged 13. Author's collection
217 Fred Gettings, 'Abstract Relief'. Private collection

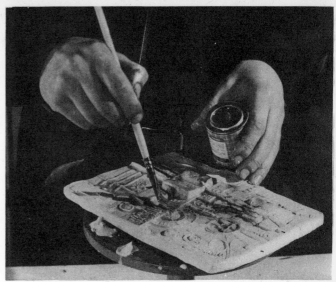

218

218 'Funny Man', by Pat Pitman, aged 11 and Elaine Crawford, aged 7.
Author's collection

219 Trewin Copplestone, 'Abstract Cast'. Artist's collection

220 Trewin Copplestone, 'The Black Circle'. Artist's collection

219

textures on your own block, as I suggested, you will see some of the advantages and disadvantages of different types of textures and patterns, and you will therefore have a better idea which textures to use when you proceed to the finished work of art.

By now you should be in a position to make a finished cast. Make another block of plasticine and then texture it in any way you think fit. Make the deepest impressions first – possibly by pressing in the ends of a wooden stick which will reproduce in the form of blocks – then texture the rest of the surface with patterns of a more superficial nature. When you feel that your design is worth casting build up the wall around it, and pour in the liquid plaster as before. When the cast is dry you can remove it and file it down at the edges if you so wish. A final coating of varnish often enhances the appearance of the cast, particularly so if the varnish is applied liberally so as to settle in the deeper areas of the cast leaving an uneven 'glaze' on the surface (plate 217).

If you so wish you can colour your plaster slightly before you make the cast as this takes away the stark whiteness of the original colour, and, if done cleverly, can add a rather nice quality to the finished product. There are various methods of colouring – you can mix with the plaster a few spoonsfull of paint water which, when thoroughly mixed into the plaster, adds an overall tone; or you can sprinkle a few pinches of powder paint into the plaster when you have finished mixing it. This last method produces chance splashes of colour on the surface of the cast which can be very beautiful. Another equally satisfactory method is to leave one or two flecks of powder on the plasticine prior to pouring in the liquid plaster of Paris. This has the advantage of ensuring that the colour stains the surface of the cast instead of being completely lost in the interior of the plaster.

The cast in plate 217 was coloured by leaving flecks of colour powder on the plasticine, and by the application of two liberal coats of oak varnish. The cast *Funny Man* on plate 218, which was made jointly by two children in my studio, was coloured with a layer of wood stainer.

The cast by Trewin Copplestone (plate 219) was made on a clay base. The circles were made by pressing in the ends of a round pole, copper piping and rings, whilst the semi-

114

circular shapes to the right were made by dragging the end
of a ruler in the clay. This effect can only be achieved in
clay as plasticine is not resilient enough for the purpose. The
hexagonal shapes were made by pressing in a carved piece
of wood. Care was taken to make sure that the angles made
by these shapes were slightly different so that they would
catch the light and reflect it to the eyes in slightly varying
intensities. The whole cast was painted in silver so as to
enhance the reflecting quality of the design.

The lovely painted cast *The Black Circle* also by Copplestone,
(plate 220), was made in quite a different way. The
projecting squares, ovals and circles were 'pre-cast' and then
set into a bed of wet plaster. The tops of these projections
were painted in oil colour directly onto the unprepared
plaster surface. It would be a good idea for you to attempt a
similar design for yourself in the technique we have just
examined, but you will find that although it is technically easy
to make a similar cast it is very difficult indeed to produce
a pleasant design as there are so many different factors
to be taken into account during its construction. There must
be a balance not merely between the number of projections

and the plain surface but also between the sizes and heights and shapes of the projections themselves.

There is no reason why one should always produce 'abstract' work in plaster. The many beautiful seal casts made in Persia, Babylon and India are produced by a method not substantially different from the one we have just examined. The cast of soldiers made by a thirteen-year-old boy on plate 216 was made by casting in clay an impression left by ordinary tin soldiers. It would be quite possible to make similar reproductions by modelling in reverse into a piece of plasticine or clay, and then making a cast which can, if required, be turned into a master-cast. If you wish to make many copies of a particular model you will find that it is more satisfactory to make a fresh mould in plasticine each time rather than to try using the same mould each time. If your first cast is satisfactory all you need do is press in a block of plasticine and you will have a new mould ready for casting.

If one wishes to work in any large size, plaster will prove to be impractical and reinforced concrete will have to be used. The four-foot-high statue in plate 223 was made from concrete in precisely the same way as the abstract cast (plate 217). Once the first layer of concrete had been poured into the clay mould I pushed in a stout iron rod and some chicken wire which was then sandwiched between another layer of concrete. On top of this second layer I placed another layer of metal rods and chicken wire to reinforce the concrete, and poured over the third and final layer of concrete. Whilst the back of the statue was still wet and the whole cast in its mould I smoothed down the back and gave it a texture with clock springs, cogs and other brick-à-brac so that the statue would look pleasant from the back as well as from the front.

221-
222 Indian Seals from Mohenjodaro. By courtesy of the Trustees of the British Museum, London

223 Fred Gettings, 'Standing Figure', concrete. Private collection

Modelling

224-
226 Making wax sculpture

The making of small free-standing forms from different materials can be a most enjoyable way of learning how to appreciate sculpture. The simplest method I know is that of building up figures out of old match-sticks and candle wax.

Stick two or three matches through a matchbox and then drop hot wax from a lighted candle onto them and press another match into the wax. Repeat the operation until you have a simple but structurally sound archway, and then, using this arch as a basis for a simple structure, start building out a tangle of matches 'cemented' together with wax until they form a pleasant abstract form. Several problems will present themselves to you after a while – one is of balance: not merely compositional balance, but physical balance, because the matchbox base is not very heavy and therefore tends to tip over easily. The problem is for you to build your forms so that they balance on the matchbox without overturning it. You could, of course, pin down the matchbox onto a piece of wood, but this would be evading the problem which will be instructive to solve.

Once you have made one or two figures in wax and match-sticks you may wish to graduate to old nails, bits of scrap iron and some hardeners like plastic metal, Araldite or Cataloy Paste. There is no reason why you should use expensive welding equipment to make small figures like the one by Cesar on plate 227. A smaller version of this sculpture could be made out of pieces of tin welded together with Cataloy Paste.

The crucifix figure on plate 228 was made by modelling Polyfilla on to a fine-wire armature. The armature was built from coiled wire which had been wrapped around a length of strong wire until the basic shape of the figure had been sketched out. When the armature was completed a small quantity of Polyfilla was mixed on a glass palette and smoothed into the wire framework with a modelling tool. This operation was repeated until the whole of the wire armature was covered by a layer of plaster. The figure was then sanded down and painted.

Plasticine savours of our childhood, not merely in its association with school where cheap materials are ever popular, but also as part of that innocent attitude to art where permanence is not a criterion of a work of art. Since plasticine is such an adaptable material in that it may be

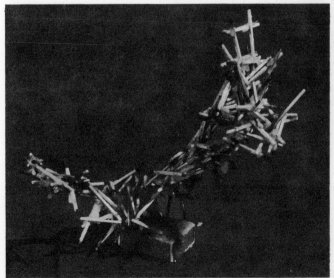

227

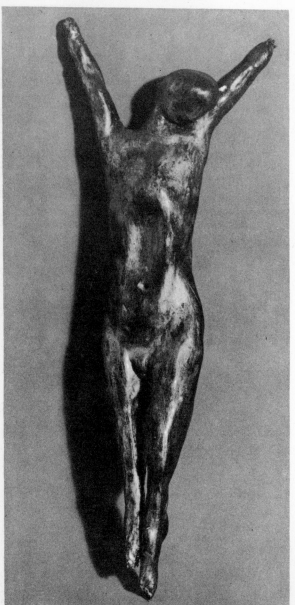

228

used for models from a life-size head to the smallest button
mould, and because it does not need continual attention like
clay, which needs to be dampened frequently, it is the ideal
material for the sort of experimental work with which we
are concerned in this book.

As a medium its chief drawback is that it tends to become
soft with constant handling, but to a certain extent this can
be overcome by working it with a modelling tool, and
avoiding actual contact with warm fingers. When working
in plasticine it is best to use a sheet of plate glass or metal
as a base, particularly when modelling in relief, so that the
plasticine will adhere firmly to its anchorage.

There are now on the market several kinds of modelling
materials which resemble in consistency and modelling
potential such permanent plastics as plasticine and Aloplast,
and which, unlike these two, dry stone-hard. They are sold
commercially under the names of Pyruma and Plastone and
may be obtained in most large stores. They are neither as
easy to handle or as aesthetically satisfying from a tactile
point of view as plasticine, but if one cannot rid oneself of
the prejudice that a work of art should be permanent one
has no alternative but to use them for modelling.

Both these clays are self-hardening and have an exceptional
resistance to heat. They set in a stone-like substance which
has a very pleasing colour and texture. They are useful
clays for coiled pottery work, pressed shapes, slab pottery
and mosaic work where no kiln is available for firing, and
although they do not lend themselves to detailed work, they
may be modelled in much the same way as plasticine.
Although they both dry to a hard (and brittle) stone they can
be 'fired' at low temperatures in an ordinary oven and
thereby rendered even harder.

When modelling with either of these two clays there is a
very important point to remember: they tend to shrink. If
you are modelling something of any length, say a figure of a
man, and you lay this figure down on its back to dry you
will find that due to drying contraction the figure will
easily crack at the weakest point – in this instance, most likely
the neck. There are two ways to avoid this: the figure could
be placed on a sheet of slightly oiled glass or on a 'bed' of
thin slivers of wood (match-sticks will do) which have been
laid side by side with gaps of about one match between each

227 César, 'The Man of St. Denis'. Reproduced by courtesy of the Trustees
    of the Tate Gallery, London

228 Gerald Speck, 'Crucifix Figure'. Author's collection

230 'Pinched Head' by Stephen Grimsley aged 13, Author's collection

230

231

232

233

of them all along the length of the figure. When the figure contracts both these arrangements allow it to slide and cohere rather than to pull one part against another and break. When using the match-stick method you must allow your figure to dry just a little before placing it on its bed, otherwise the match-sticks will make an impression on its back. Because of its marked tendency to contract in drying, armature work is not suitable. Sometimes minute cracks will appear on the surface of figures modelled in these self-hardening clays. These can be obliterated by damping the area and pressing in fresh clay to fill up the cracks. Very large cracks indicate that the structure is probably weak, and the figure should be thrown away as useless.

There are very many different types of clay for making pottery. All of them are formed by the decomposition of felspathic rocks due to the erosive action of vegetation, water and carbonic acid in the soil. The primary clay of kaolin or 'china clay' is the purest form obtained from sedimentary beds, whereas the secondary clays, ranging from the refractory silica clays, vitreous 'ball clays' and the fusible tertiary clays, are obtained from deposits which have been carried away from their original beds. Whatever the colour, texture or consistency of the different clays they are all made of the same basic material – hydrated silicate of alumina. All the differences, particularly those of colour, arise from the quantities of silica, lime, iron and organic matters with which they are mixed.

Clays need careful processing and a long period of time in 'maturing' before they are suitable for pottery work. For this reason it is not possible to use the clays one finds in one's own locality. Only very rarely is it possible to find a 'tertiary' clay deposit which may be used for pottery, and even then it is necessary to clean it by sieving and allow it to weather for a year or so. Quite obviously, the best thing to do is to buy your clay ready prepared. You should buy your clays in half hundredweight amounts direct from a reputable pottery or a potter's supplier. Most art shops sell small rolls of clay but they are extremely expensive in such small quantities.

When clay is 'fired' at temperatures a little over 1000°C it turns into pottery. Its change is not merely a physical change due to hardening through loss of moisture as in the

234

235   236

case of Plastone and Pyruma, but a chemical change of a highly complex nature. Once it has been fired it will retain its shape for ever, but until that time it is extremely brittle and fragile. It is therefore not recommended to model in clay unless you intend to fire the finished product.

The chief difficulty with clay modelling is that one needs a kiln, for only a kiln can give the regulated temperatures and conditions for the production of good pottery. Because kilns are expensive, and because the processes involved in kiln work such as glazing and firing are so complicated, I make no attempt to discuss pottery in this book except in the broadest terms and then only in so far as a pottery technique is applicable to clays which do not need firing. Anyone who is fortunate enough to live near a pottery is advised to pay a visit to it both to examine the fascinating process behind pottery making, and to find out the cost of hiring a kiln, and, if possible, working space. Most potteries offer a course of simple instruction in actual pottery techniques and hire out kilns for both the biscuit and glaze stage of firing. It will be more convenient and probably a little cheaper to use the equipment, clays, glazes and wheels at the pottery than to complete the pre-firing preparations at home and then transport the object to the pottery for its firing.

In principle the form of your model in clay may be structurally the same as a model in plasticine. One must bear in mind that during the firing process the clay will at one point become extremely soft, and any elongated form, or any weak structure, will droop or collapse. This is the reason why good pottery figures which appear so light and delicate, are so often placed against 'backgrounds' of foliage or some such structural device.

A good way to begin experimental work with modelling clays is to make one or two relief models. Because this is the simplest technical approach to modelling it is an excellent way of getting a 'feel' for the materials, to discover their potentialities and improve your ability.

The simplest relief method consists of 'drawing' a picture in lengths and blocks of clay onto a large flat piece of clay as Peter Stockbridge has done in plate 234, but a more interesting method is to model large 'half round' forms, like the Benin plaque at plate 237.

Press a lump of plasticine onto your sheet of glass and mould it into a rough shape such as a square or a circle. Choose some simple motif which you would like to model.

Block out the main areas of your design first because this will enable you to judge whether or not you are establishing the right proportions between the raised areas of plasticine and the lower areas. You can then proceed to the more detailed modelling of smoothing the surface or adding patterns and textures, but only when you are satisfied with the design as a whole. Even when you move on to the detailed work do not model in one little area for a long time but try to let the design move together towards completion as a whole. An exercise which you might choose to undertake, and which would be very rewarding, would be to make a relief model copy of a Greek coin or a Renaissance medallion.

Should you wish to transfer your relief model to plaster you will have first of all to establish whether it is suitable for such a process. The raised shapes must be sloping, flowing mountain-like from the lower areas without any undercutting in their sides. If this is not the case, and the design cannot be adapted without being spoiled, then your relief cannot be transferred to plaster, for although it would be quite easy to make a cast of the reverse of the mould in which the raised areas will be depressed and vice versa, it will not be possible to make a cast of the mould itself, as any undercut in the matrix will act as a lock to the second cast. The Benin plaque would cast easily (and in fact its present form *is* a cast), whereas the 'Saxon' would not cast at all.

If your relief model is adaptable for casting you must build a plasticine wall around the relief to take the plaster of Paris. When you have poured in a strong mix of plaster you can brush the sides of the mould with a soft brush to tickle away the air bubbles. Allow the mould to dry and remove the plasticine relief. The mould may now be used for pressing in plasticine to make many copies or for pressing in one of the self-hardening clays which will make a durable copy.

If you wish to spend some time making a work of art with some utility you might care to manufacture a set of draughtsmen by modelling some abstract design onto a piece of plasticine the size and shape of an ordinary

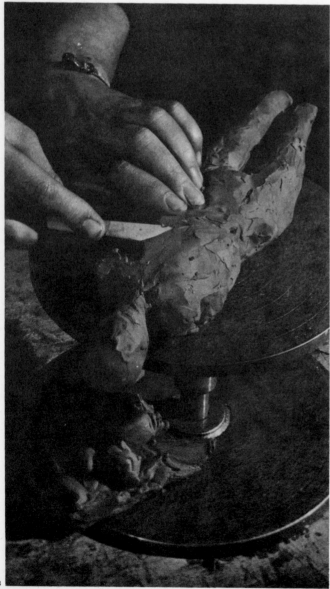

241

242

draughtsman, and make a matrix in plaster of your design. It will be an easy matter for you to make twenty-four copies by pressing in pieces of Pyruma and afterwards sanding them down on the bottom to make them smooth.

A more ambitious undertaking in relief work would be to make a fair copy of the Benin plaque (plate 237). Model the simple massive shapes of the three figures as carefully as possible, ensuring that there is no undercutting around the difficult areas of the face and headgear. Do not incise the decorative circles on the background or the chain-link armour on the bodies, for this decorative work would look much better in reverse, as a delicately raised linear marking. When you have made your plaster matrix you can scratch these decorative patterns into the hard plaster of Paris using a similar technique to the one discussed on page 110, and these will reproduce beautifully when the clay is pressed into the matrix.

The Polynesian figure on plate 235 may suggest a suitable relief for an ash tray. As a figure it would best be tackled by making a plasticine model of its back, of which a cast is then taken in plaster. You can then press into this matrix a layer of clay and model the body of the man in complete confidence that the back will come out perfectly when the whole is allowed to dry. The head could be modelled as a separate entity, and then stuck onto the projecting neck with a little moisture.

The figure on plate 239 is a small project for a crucified Christ which was to be executed in concrete. Although it is in theory a model in the round since it was intended to go against a wall, it was conceived as a relief. As the preparatory modelling stage at plate 238 suggests, the figure was built up as a whole, and no part was allowed to develop without being integrated with the rest. The final texture was obtained by pitting the figure with knife cuts, match-sticks and screws.

Mosaic work is really a kind of relief modelling. The word 'mosaic' is derived ultimately from the Greek meaning 'apertaining to the Muses', and therefore 'ornamental, decorative and artistic'. Even now, in its very widest sense the word may be applied to any work which consists of a plane surface of juxtaposed shapes and colours.

We have already seen that a fine mosaic can be made

243

from pieces of gummed paper, as on plate 186, and in fact almost any material may be used, though marble, glass or natural stones united by a mastic cement are the most common. The size, extent and utility of mosaics can vary enormously from the tiny intricate brooches of the Ancient Egyptians to the massive mosaic pavements of the Romans, and from the abstract formal designs of the Byzantines to the 'reproductions' of Titian's and Giorgione's paintings made in the fifteenth century in Italy.

Although pieces of mosaic (or *tesserae*, as they are called) can be purchased in shops, it is possible and even preferable to make one's own from one of the self-hardening clays such as Plastone. The method is quite simple. A lump of Plastone is rolled flat by rolling a stick over it with two slats of wood on either side, to ensure uniform thickness, as in plate 241, and then a sheet of plate glass is pressed over the Plastone surface in order to give it a smooth texture. Strips of Plastone are then cut by resting a straight edge across the wooden slats and drawing a sharp oiled knife along the clay, and then cutting in a similar way at right angles to the original cut. The size and shape of the mosaic

pieces will vary in terms of the size and shape of the design you intend to execute. The pieces should be allowed to dry in normal conditions for a week or so and then, if possible, they should be placed in an oven and dried for about half an hour at a fairly high temperature.

There are two different ways of colouring the *tesserae*. If you wish to prepare a large number of them in one colour it is possible to tint the Plastone before actually making the pieces by mixing powder colour into it whilst still soft. One must be careful not to use too much colour or the quality of the clay may be spoiled. Also if you do colour the *tesserae* in this way do not heat the finished pieces excessively or the powder colour will be affected adversely by the heat and become discoloured. The *tesserae* may be permanently coloured individually by mixing Araldite (obtained in hardware stores) in small quantities and making a solution of it with turpentine. This is then used as a liquid mix for powder paint. The colour dries very hard, almost enamel-like, is extremely durable, and neither cracks nor fades. The copy of Chinese Key Money at plate 245 was painted in this way several years ago.

245

246

Another way of making mosaic pieces is by breaking up pottery, glass and stones (plate 240).

Before work on a design is begun it is necessary to prepare a board on which to work. A shallow tray is made by nailing thin strips of wood around the perimeter of a piece of plywood the size of the working area of your design. Only three of the sides should be nailed down at this point, but a fourth should be made ready. This tray should then be placed on your working desk with the wall-less side towards you, and you should begin to work in the following way. The design is built up by laying a strip of cement (Tiluma is recommended, ordinary plaster of Paris will not suffice) and pressing in the *tesserae* side by side with a sufficient pressure to squeeze a quantity of cement between them. The cement which appears over the top of the mosaic surface can be removed with a damp cloth. It is advisable to work the mosaic in small areas at a time so as to prevent a large expanse of cement hardening before the *tesserae* have been pushed in.

The finished mosaics can be given a coat of clear varnish if Araldite has been used for the colouring. If powder colour

244 'Doves drinking at a bowl'. Galla Placidia, Ravenna

245 Copy of Chinese key money painted in Araldite by Fred Gettings. Original in the Department of Numismatics, British Museum

246 Byzantine Madonna and Child, Mosaic in Sant' Apollinare Nuovo, Ravenna

247

248

249

was mixed directly with the clay a coating of a hard wax may be applied.

The lovely mosaic at plates 244 and 246 may suggest to you a design which you could adapt to your own purposes. In really great mosaic work, such as the mosaics at Ravenna, not only the colour and the formalised pattern, but even the angle at which each individual *tessera* is set plays an important part in the overall effect.

By now you should be in a position to move on to modelling in the round. The chief fault of the beginner has a curious parallel in the history of art. At the time of the early Renaissance, when the Italians were re-discovering the Greek and Roman ideal of beauty, sculpture of any substantial size was conceived chiefly as an appendage to architecture, and was concerned with the decoration of wall surfaces and buildings. As a result of this the form of most sculpture was conceived in terms of high or low relief, and even full-length statues were placed in little alcoves. Thus, as we might have expected, when the Italians created the first free-standing figures along classical lines they were conceived primarily as figures to be seen from the front, as

if they were still in niches in the walls. Most beginners in sculpture and modelling tend to think in precisely these terms – they conceive their figures from one point of view only, usually from the front.

Obviously, any object which is modelled in the round must be aesthetically satisfying from every point of view. A test of a really fine piece of free-standing sculpture is that it can be looked at from every angle and still be interesting to the eye. The five photographs of the Dahomey figure plates 247-251 illustrate how the general shape of the whole figure is retained through the figure and yet a sufficient variety of pattern in silhouetted form is preserved to make each viewpoint unique and interesting. As the statue is only seven inches high the African sculptor has been careful to design it so that it presents an interesting series of shapes and patterns even when examined from above.

The first point which must be borne in mind when making a free-standing model, then, is that it must be looked at from every angle. Whilst one is modelling a figure one must be continually turning it round to see how it is developing *as a whole*. There is a simple modelling stand for

250

251

247-
251 'Dahomey Figure', 19th century. Private collection

such a purpose, and if you have any intention of doing a large amount of modelling such a stand would be a worthwhile investment. A rough and ready modelling stand can be made from a block of wood with a hole in its centre and a flat piece of board with a projecting length of circular wood which slots into the hole in the block, but the smooth-running modelling stand is to be preferred.

The model must be built up step by step. If one were making, for example, a model of a head (plate 253), one would first of all establish the main form even to the extent of constructing a skeletal relationship of internal forms and then adding muscle groups to give the external form. Once the basic form has been established, work must begin on the individual forms which make up the larger composition. Do not worry at this stage about texture, for a lively surface texture will develop as the modelling tool searches for the form. All the time you are working on your model you should be turning your board this way and that so as to catch as many viewpoints as possible. Your aim should be to have a simple sculptural theme which should be immediately evident, and yet contain sufficient variety of outline to

129

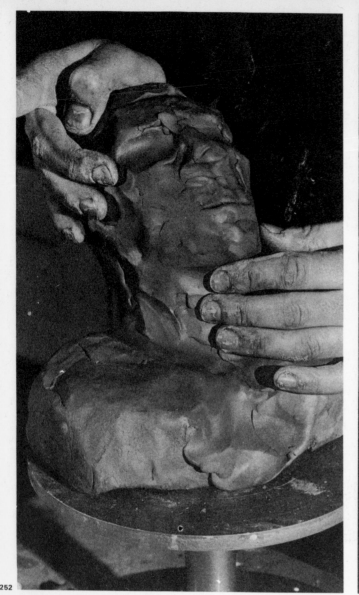

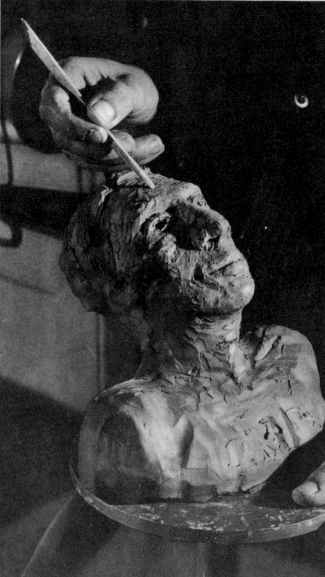

252

render the basic form interesting. This point can best be clarified by pointing to a definite illustration. The four different angles of *Eve* (plates 254-257) have at first glance the same visual impact, for one is immediately aware of a *curled-up form* no matter from what angle one examines it. But within the limitations of this one form there are a wealth of variations in the rhythms and textures which prevent the model from ever becoming boring. There is a liveliness about the figure both in execution and design which makes it a very satisfying work of art. The figure is asleep, not dead like the Christ in plate 239. The starkness of the Christ was as much a demand of the subject matter as the lively treatment, soft rhythm and formal tensions are demanded by the subject matter of *Eve*.

There are three simple pottery techniques which may be used either separately or in combination to make 'pots' or free-standing figures.

The simplest of these techniques is called 'pinching' and as its name implies it is a method of modelling by pinching and moulding clay with the fingers. It is the most elementary of modelling methods, but very satisfying to do. Usually a

'pinched' pot or model gains in rich character what it looses in beauty. One's aim in making a pinched model should be to catch a certain spontaneity of shape, freshness of vision and freedom of technique rather than to produce a laboured and well-finished work. The little head on plate 259 is a lovely example of pinched modelling, for it is possible to see how each part of the face, such as the eyes or mouth, have been made directly with finger pressures.

'Coiling' is another popular pottery technique, and is particularly suitable for large pots and figures whose size prohibit throwing. The pot is built out of lengths of rolled clay which are pressed together. Coarse groggy sand and Plastone are suitable for coil work. It is advisable to work at a turntable. First model the base, which need not be coiled but can be made from a flat piece of clay cut to the size and shape you intend the bottom of your pot to be. It should be at least half an inch thicker than the sides of the pot will be as you have to cut the pot from the turntable with a piece of wire, rather like cutting cheese, and this will take a considerable slice off the bottom. The rolls of clay for the coiling are prepared by taking a larger sausage of clay and

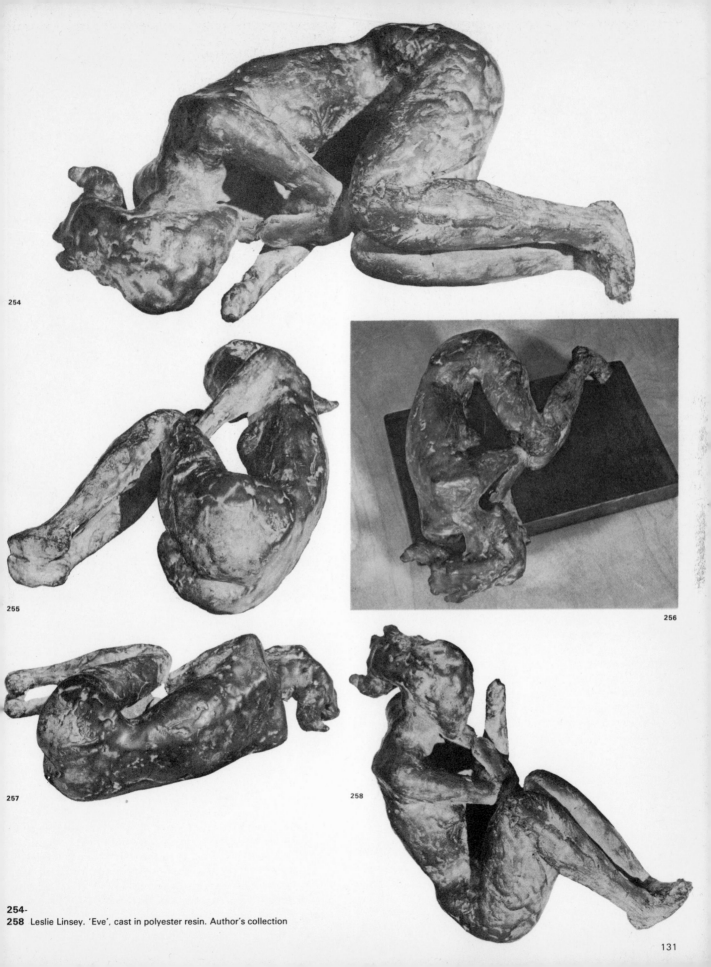

254

255

256

257

258

254-
258 Leslie Linsey. 'Eve', cast in polyester resin. Author's collection

259 'Pinched Head' by Stephen Grimsley, aged 13. Author's collection

260 Making a coiled pot

rolling it backwards and forwards on a board with the palm of your hands until it is about two feet in length and approximately half an inch in diameter. Lengths of clay over two feet are difficult to roll, and there is a tendency for them to become 'knotty' or of unequal diameter throughout their length. Rolling is best done quickly, and in one firm motion of the hand so that the backward and forward motion of the hands allows the clay to roll from the base of the fingers to their tips: the hollow of the palm tends to make the roll uneven. The finished coil should be of even thickness throughout its length, rather like a piece of rope. One should prepare several of these coils before beginning work on an actual model, and the ones not in use should be kept under a damp cloth so that they will stay moist.

The coiled pot is built by winding the rolls of clay around on top of each other and pressing the top layer into the second, so that the pot shape looks rather like a flattened spring. One can either build up each coil separately, completing one circuit of the shape at a time so that the pot is made from a series of rings, or one can allow each roll to wind on over itself until it is completely used up. Spiral

rolling lends itself more easily to bellied shapes of ewers, and they tend to break less easily before the firing.

Each time several rings have been built up the sides must be smoothed in as firmly as possible to make them compact, taking care not to trap air in any of the grooves whilst smoothing down. Water should not be used to stick the coils together – and if this is found to be at all necessary the clay is not of a correct consistency for coil work.

Plate 262 is a fine example of coiled pottery.

The Kwale figure on plate 261 is the obvious sort of figure for coil and pinch work. The body could easily be made by coiling thin lengths of clay around a thin stick, and then afterwards smoothing the inside with a long modelling tool, as shown in plate 266. The head and feet could be pinched into shape and pressed into the coiled body. As the feet would not support the body whilst still wet you could either support the figure underneath with a small block of wood or clay, or the whole figure could be laid on its back with its feet in the air until the clay dries.

Slab pottery is the third method for simple figure making. A flat sheet of clay is rolled and then cut into lengths as in

261

plate 264. The sides of each slab of clay may be bevelled with a knife so as to make the slab join easily to the next (plate 265). The slab pot which is being made in the series of illustrations has five sides. When the sides have been joined together in this way the shape should be stood on its end, and the inner seams between the slabs should be smoothed down with a long stick or modelling tool so that there is no danger of the shapes splitting from one another during the drying process (plate 266). A small slab should be added to the bottom at this stage, and one can smooth down the sides of the pot and add to its compactness by hitting the sides firmly with a flat stick of wood. Although it is obviously more practical to work in lengths of five or six inches for pottery shapes as narrow as the one illustrated, there is no limit, within reason, to the height of the finished article. One can build one, two or even three stories on top of the first by preparing other shapes along the lines of the first and then fixing them firmly on top. This junction may be left as an intrinsic part of the pot shape or smoothed down so as to leave the pot with one continuous smooth outline. Decoration can be added afterwards either by attaching decorative relief slabs to the walls (made by the process described on page 109) or by modelling directly onto sides of the pot as in plate 269.

The quaint dog on plate 263 was made from a tubular slab of clay which was given a 'fur' texture by pressing clay through a fine sieve and sticking it on to the tubular body. The tail, head and legs were pinched shapes which were added when the body was completed.

Certain shapes are very easy to cast and therefore are suitable for manufacturing in quantity. Supposing you set out to make a piggy-bank of pottery or Plastone like the one on plate 273 and you like its shape so much that you decide to make some more – perhaps to give as Christmas presents for your friends – it would save a great deal of time to make a mould of your original pig and cast several from this one instead of modelling each one individually.

The first thing to do would be to make a plasticine model of the pig or animal you wish to reproduce, and then examine it to see how best it can be cast. Obviously, if one is making a two-piece mould (which is the simplest for a free standing figure) one must be able to lift the figure free from

262

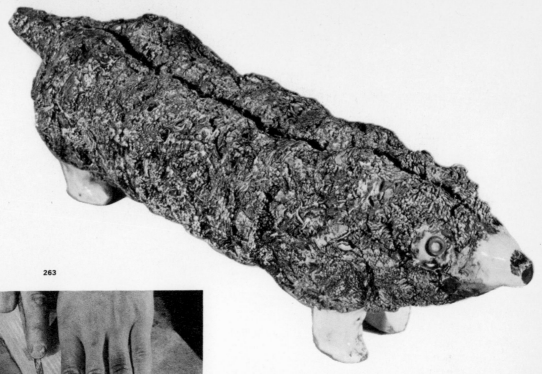

263

261 Kwale Figure. By courtesy of the Trustees of the British Museum, London

262 Coiled pot. Author's collection

263 'Textured Dog'. Author's collection

264
269 Making slab pottery

266

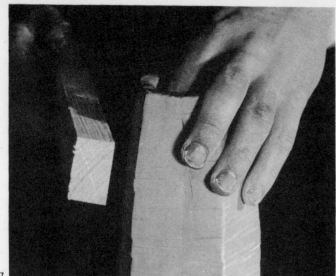

267

268

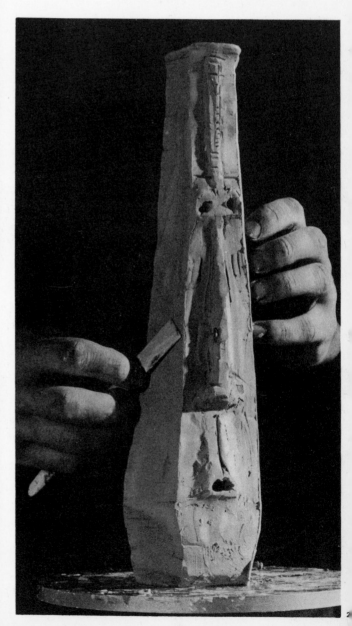

136

271 Chinese pottery pleasure pavilion grave object, Han dynasty. By courtesy of the Trustees of the British Museum, London

270 Face vase from the Sepik area, New Guinea. Museum of Ethnology, Munich

270

271

272

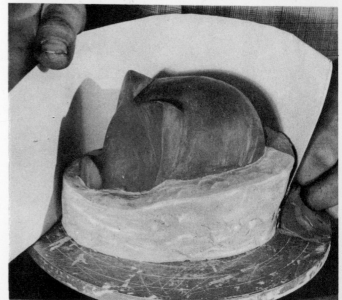

both moulds without damaging it and yet have a 'seam' which neither weakens the figure structurally nor is awkward to obliterate in the final stages of the casting. In the case of the pig on plate 273 the seam line would have to run around the fattest part of its body, curve down slightly where the ears protrude gently from the front legs and then run along the middle of his mouth. With such a junction between the two moulds one would have little trouble in lifting the two castings out, and there would be a sufficient area for the two pieces to join together firmly.

Once the seam line has been determined you must build a plasticine block around the figure so that a platform runs at right angles to its sides following the seam line you had determined (plate 274). Around this platform you must next build a wall so that the protruding half of your figure is contained in a shallow pit. The wall may be built out of cardboard or plasticine, but it must be strong enough to stand the weight of the plaster, and it must be completely watertight. Plaster should now be prepared in the usual way (see page 108) and poured into the pit. When the plaster is dry the plasticine platform and the cardboard sides are removed (plate 275) and the figure is turned over on its back and the other side cast in a similar fashion. A coating of shellac on the exposed platform surface of the first plaster mould will prevent the two plaster surfaces from sticking together. When this second mould is dry you will have two moulds which between them cover the whole surface of your figure.

Clay or Plastone reproductions can now be made by pressing slabs of clay into each mould in turn and sliding a knife over the platform edge of the mould, as in plate 276. Leave the clay shapes in the mould for a few hours so that they dry and shrink a little as this will make them a little easier to remove. They should then be taken out and joined together with a little slip brushed on the edges, as in plate 277. If there are any deficiencies in the surface of your model you should add pieces of clay and smooth them out at this stage, for once the model is dry, major deficiencies cannot be remedied. If your figure is intended to be a moneybox then you must slice out the hole in its back wide enough to take coins. Now set your figure aside for a few days to dry and carry on preparing the others.

278

When the figures are dry you can sandpaper them smooth, or leave a slight texture, as required. If they are of clay you should have them biscuited. Plastone figures may be painted at this stage with coloured Araldite.

It is, of course, always possible to make a cast of a basic shape and add other pieces later. Take the lovely African Hyena figure on plate 278, for example: it would be very difficult to cast it in anything less than a five or six piece mould in its present form, but if you were to make a two pieces mould of its body, legs and head in a similar fashion to your pig moulds you could then add the tail, ears and toes after the casting process. The pleasant texture on this particular figure was obtained by pressing a match end into the clay whilst still soft and then, when the figure was dry, running an almost dry brush of dark pigment over its surface so that the colour was caught on the raised portions but missed on the impressions made by the matchstick.

278 Hyena, Africa. By courtesy of the Trustees of the British Museum, London

279 Klee, 'Senecio'. Kupferstichkabinett, Kunstmuseum, Basel © S.P.A.D.E.M. Paris, 1965

280 Masaccio, 'Virgin and Child'. Reproduced by courtesy of the Trustees of the National Gallery, London

Conclusion

Art is an immense search for knowledge, inward or outward. A work of art, a painting or a statue, is the outward form of this search, the material manifestation of something which is essentially an inner and spiritual activity. Therefore, it is the activity of art itself and not the end product of this activity, which is really important, in that it depends on a true inner evaluation of experiences.

The history of art is really the history of the evolution of man's changing vision as recorded in the material forms of his art. In seeing, in attempting to learn to be artists, we are participating in an age-old mystery, by which our own reality is constructed. Masaccio's pictures are the embodiment of an idea which changed man's visions and beliefs about the fundamental nature of the world around him: after Masaccio the world was seen in depth, and the medieval world of flat patterns disappeared for several hundred years. Even today we see the world around us a little through the eyes of Masaccio. For we ourselves are part of the new vision created by the spiritual Odyssey of the Renaissance some five centuries ago: the way to see the world and interpret its complexities was determined long before our birth. In the early part of this century the questions and answers inspired by the Bauhaus experiments in Germany enabled us to see things differently again through the eyes of Gropius and Klee. This means that our whole vision, our interpretation of reality, is a complex structure built on the understanding of artists long dead or still living. Every artist who ever lived and worked lives in us. We, or rather, our vision and our understanding, are the products of twenty thousand years of art, the temporary crystallization of an ever-changing interpretation of the nature of reality.

By participating in this ever-changing way of seeing, we are learning about ourselves and about the external world. By learning how to see and how to live, we are being artists. We have to be artists to survive.

List of materials and methods

The principal references are on the following pages:

Photographic credits

Michael Holford:
Plates 1, 2, 9, 15, 16, 19, 20, 25, 28, 33, 35, 36, 38, 40, 50, 106, 111, 114, 116, 118, 143, 158, 169, 184, 186, 188, 190, 191, 195, 196, 198, 219, 220, 228, 234, 245, 260, 272, 273.

James Holt:
Plates 4, 5, 13, 22-24, 30-32, 34, 41, 43-48, 56, 58-60, 67, 69, 126, 129, 131, 133, 138, 145-147, 149-157, 163-165, 167, 168, 170-172, 175-177, 179-181, 192-194, 197, 200-215, 218, 224-226, 230, 238, 239, 241-243, 247-259, 262-269, 274-277.

Helen Piers:
Plates 6, 7, 11, 14, 21, 26, 27, 42, 51-54, 61, 68, 107, 117, 125, 136, 216, 217, 223, 229, 240.